Editorial

Bairns not Bombs

John Ainslie dissects Trident

Sometimes I would ring Scottish CND and John Ainslie would answer. He was a man of few words on the phone, but he always responded swiftly and positively to requests to print his work in *The Spokesman* journal. So it is with renewed gratitude that we publish this collection of his work dissecting the intricacies of the flotilla of nuclear armed and powered submarines based some 40 miles from Glasgow. Most of the articles were written a decade or more ago, so events have moved on. But the essential threat of mass death endures and is, indeed, being updated with new submarines—hence the new missile compartment being shipped from the United States to Britain (see cover). John would surely have asked whether this sizeable structure would fit properly in the submarine currently being built in Barrow.

Trident missiles on Royal Navy submarines, we are told, are tasked to deliver multiple hydrogen bombs on targets in and around Moscow and elsewhere in Russia. The missiles are leased from the United States, which deploys many more on its own submarines based on the Atlantic and Pacific coasts. Trident missiles on submarines based in Scotland are much closer to the perceived Russian enemy. Proximity matters, even for intercontinental ballistic missiles.

Interestingly, John Ainslie refers to the discussions in Britain in 1963 about where to base Polaris, the US ICBM that preceded Trident. A couple of years earlier, in 1961, when US Polaris submarines were to be serviced from Holy Loch, it generated enormous public opposition in Britain. Bertrand Russell, with many others in attendance, fixed a notice of disapproval to the doors of the Ministry of Defence in Whitehall, outside which he sat on the cold pavement. Later, simultaneous sit-down protests took place in London and at Holy Loch, with numerous arrests. In due course, British submarines supplanted US ones. That arrangement continues. The United States supplies the missiles and launch compartment and, as Ainslie's work reveals, much of the computer software as well as some of the hardware for the warheads, which are assembled in Britain. This 'special' relationship continues to shape British politics.

'Bairns not Bombs' invokes concern for our children. John Ainslie and colleagues readily donned the green t-shirts. Some years on, our times grow more menacing as nuclear threats are made and answered by Russia and the United States while the war in Ukraine continues. The military buildup increases, including new generations of nuclear-armed submarines. Some influential voices, such as the Secretary General of the United Nations, speak out against this dangerous direction in world affairs. To encourage and strengthen those voices, we urgently need more insights such as those afforded by John Ainslie's painstaking analysis, as well as learning from the example of his courageous activism.

* * *

Christopher Farley

Chris Farley has left his clear and unmistakable handwriting on many files of the Bertrand Russell Peace Foundation from its early decades in the 1960s and '70s. He won Bertrand Russell's trust. We pay tribute to Chris and his work following his death in December 2022.

Tony Simpson

▼ From the *Glasgow Herald*, 02/06/1992

The Spokesman

Bairns Not Bombs: *John Ainslie dissects Trident*
Edited by Tony Simpson and Tom Unterrainer

Published by Spokesman for the
Bertrand Russell Peace Foundation
Ken Coates: Editor 1970 to 2010

Spokesman 153   2023

CONTENTS

Editorial	3	
The UK-US nuclear nexus *Insights from the Ainslie Archive*	5	*Tim Street*
Nuclear Dependency *Arguments from* The Future of the British Bomb	11	*John Ainslie*
Trident: Nowhere to Go	20	*John Ainslie*
Disarming Trident	37	*John Ainslie*
The Cuban Missile Crisis	51	*John Ainslie*
Substandard *The Trident whistleblower and the safety of British submarines*	59	*John Ainslie*
If Britain fired Trident	83	*John Ainslie*
Sword of Damocles	99	*Trish Whitham, Janet Fenton, Rob Edwards, Tim Street, Peter Burt, Alan Charlton*
Christopher Farley 1934-2022	113	*Tony Simpson*
Chris Farley *An Appreciation*	116	*Russell Stetler*
Reviews	118	*Beverley Naidoo* *Ailish D'Arcy* *Helen Jackson* *Barry Baldwin* *Stephen Winfield* *Richard Corbett*

Cover: *Will it fit? How much does it cost? US-built missile compartment for Royal Navy's replacement Trident submarine, en route December 2022*

ISSN 1367 7748   ISBN 978 0 85124 9223

Subscriptions
Institutions £40.00 (ex UK)
£33.00 (UK)
Individuals £20.00 (UK)
£25.00 (ex UK)

A CIP catalogue record for this book is available from the British Library

Published by
The Bertrand Russell Peace Foundation Ltd,
5 Churchill Park,
Nottingham, NG4 2HF
England
Tel. 0115 9708318
email: editor@russfound.org
www.spokesmanbooks.org
www.russfound.org

Editorial Board
John Daniels
Kate Fleet
Stuart Holland
Henry McCubbin
Abi Rhodes
Regan Scott

Mixed Sources
Product group from well-managed forests and other controlled sources

Cert no. SGS-COC-006541
www.fsc.org
© 1996 Forest Stewardship Council

▲ John Ainslie (wearing glasses) and friends

The UK-US nuclear nexus

Insights from the Ainslie Archive

Tim Street

Tim Street is Secretary of British Pugwash and author of The Politics of Nuclear Disarmament *(Routledge, 2021). He has been working on the Ainslie Archive for the Nuclear Information Service. This is the text of a talk given at the University of Kent in June, 2022.*

John Ainslie authored twenty reports on nuclear policy, starting in 1992 with *Cracking Under Pressure*, about defects in British nuclear submarine reactors. He also collaborated with Professor Plesch, who co-organised these panels, on a 2016 report investigating how Britain relies on the US to sustain its nuclear status.

What is the Ainslie archive?

I am currently working with other members of the Nuclear Information Service team to organise John's archive. The archive consists of documents relating to the UK's nuclear weapons that John collected over several decades. He collected information from a wide range of sources, including official US and UK government files, activist correspondence, civil society reports, academic studies, photos, graphs, newsletters and media articles.

I found working on the archive interesting for the insights it provides into how John approached the varied nuclear issues he worked on. These include: UK preparations in the 1980s for Civil Defence in the event of a nuclear attack; how British military planners developed plans to target Russia with nuclear weapons, including the famed Moscow Criterion; and the purpose and location of the many nuclear weapons-related installations in the United Kingdom—both British and American.

NIS hopes that providing a platform for John's work will allow researchers to better understand British nuclear history and decision-making, and to prevent the nuclear past—and all its dangers—from being forgotten. So, my presentation today is intended to promote the Archive and invite you to access it online.

What is the Mutual Defence Agreement?

One of the topics which the Archive sheds light on is the Mutual Defence Agreement between the UK and the US. I am going to discuss John's thoughts on the agreement and relate it to NIS's own publications on the topic. For example, Peter Burt, former NIS director, explored in a 2014 briefing how the MDA is the main agreement between the UK and the US allowing co-operation on the development of nuclear weapons. Burt outlined how the MDA 'was first signed in 1958 to allow the exchange of classified nuclear information, nuclear weapon technology, and scientific expertise, with the aim of helping both nations to develop their nuclear weapons systems.'

The MDA is a formal treaty between the two nations and has been amended a number of times over its 56-year history. Most recently it has been renewed on a regular ten year cycle. This has allowed, Burt wrote, 'arrangements for the transfer of special nuclear materials and non-nuclear components of nuclear weapons.' The MDA was last renewed in 2014 when it was extended until December 2024. For Burt, British governments have pushed renewal of the Agreement through with minimal Parliamentary oversight, rather than allowing debate and discussion on the aims and consequences of renewing the treaty.

Since 2014, there have been significant developments in the nuclear weapons programmes of both the UK and the United States. For example, collaboration has taken place in nuclear warhead development and modernisation; submarine reactor design and development; exchange of special nuclear materials; warhead stockpile stewardship research; and the construction of new nuclear infrastructure. The Ainslie archive contains historical documents on each of these areas, helping us to understand their meaning and significance.

Ainslie on the Mutual Defence Agreement

Ainslie's main published thoughts on the MDA came in his report, *The Future of the British Bomb*. Here, Ainslie notably describes the MDA as one of two Anglo-American agreements—alongside the 1963 Polaris Sales Agreement—which 'constrains' British nuclear forces. In the case of the MDA, this is because 'the information and material provided by the US can only be used for mutual defence purposes'. As for the Polaris Sales Agreement, Ainslie explains that this required British nuclear forces to be assigned to NATO, except "where her Majesty's Government may decide that supreme national interests are at stake". At the same time, he also thought that 'The importance of the "assignment to NATO" of British nuclear forces is exaggerated'. This was because, he explained, 'Britain is more likely to use nuclear weapons in a bilateral Anglo-American operation than either under NATO auspices or as an independent force'.

Ainslie then identified what, for him, was the critical issue, namely, 'whether Britain could use its nuclear forces in a situation where the US was opposed to their use. If America objected then the attack would not be in both parties interest and would be in breach of the Mutual Defence Agreement. The US would be likely to use strong-arm tactics to dissuade Britain from acting.' In practice, the UK's 'technical dependence' on the US would be what would, he argued, 'constrain any independent attack'. The British nuclear weapons establishment was thus 'almost entirely dependent on the information provided' by the MDA.

For example, the Joint Atomic Information Exchange Group controls the release of US nuclear weapons design information to the UK. There are also numerous Joint Working Groups which facilitate information sharing. Subjects have included specific scientific issues such as plasma physics, radiation and nuclear materials. There are also working groups focusing on Trident itself. John described 'the flow of knowledge' being 'overwhelmingly, but not exclusively, from America to the UK.'

Nuclear targeting

In terms of technical dependence, the issue of British nuclear targeting was something Ainslie paid particular attention to. For example, the archive contains the data he collected when he was analysing whether Trident can be used without US consent and assistance and can be targeted independently of the US. Ainslie concluded that 'reliance on American software for all aspects of targeting undermines nuclear independence. Any future British nuclear weapons system will only be as independent as Washington wants it to be.'

Ainslie goes into painstaking detail in *The Future of the British Bomb* about what this means in practice. For example, he writes—in his typically terse and economical style—that:

> 'Targeting data on British Trident submarines is processed in the Fire Control System by software produced in America. This data is created in the Nuclear Operations and Targeting Centre in London. The centre relies on US software. In 2002 the Fire Control Systems on British and American Trident submarines were modified. Just before this the computers in the London targeting centre were upgraded. The American applications used for target planning and for fire control are complex and unique.'

The US could restrict how the UK could use Trident, he argued, because:

'It would be possible for US programmers to modify the software supplied to Britain, either openly or covertly.' Despite this, 'even those who operate the system may not have an accurate perception of its dependence.' He then repeats the point that 'the British Trident system is only as independent as Washington wants it to be.'

The ability of the US to restrict British nuclear use decisions has far-reaching implications. For example, the idea of an independent British bomb remains central to its political mystique and thus its reproduction. Supporters of Trident argue that whilst the UK may be dependent on the US regarding nuclear procurement, London has independence regarding the decision to detonate it. Yet, for Ainslie, this notion is greatly undermined by the control Washington has over British nuclear detonation.

Democracy, transparency and accountability

In addition to researching these topics, Ainslie sought to introduce democracy, transparency and accountability to the UK's governance of its nuclear weapons. As noted previously, the MDA is renewed every ten years. In 2004 John outlined his thoughts on why the MDA should be subject to democratic scrutiny. In June that year he wrote to Labour MP Bruce George, chair of the Defence Committee, calling on him to hold an inquiry into the renewal of the Mutual Defence Agreement and for there to be a House of Commons debate.

In the letter, Ainslie highlighted an 'explanatory memorandum' from the Foreign and Commonwealth Office, stating that 'there are no financial implications of extending the application of Article III of the 1958 Agreement'. However, his contention was that 'the history of Anglo-American nuclear co-operation has been that the flow of information from the US has been dependent on Britain maintaining a substantial research programme of its own.'

The main focus of the UK's nuclear weapons development at that time was on the design of simulations of nuclear tests given the ban on real world testing. This, for Ainslie, was the likely 'price of ongoing support from the United States' for the UK. The Atomic Weapons Establishment at Aldermaston thus substantially increased its computing power 'at considerable expense'. Peter Burt provided an update on the issue of computer testing in his 2014 report, stating that 'the peer review arrangements' provided by the MDA have provided an 'opportunity' for the US to learn from the UK's 'experience with projects' where the latter's 'schedule is running ahead' of the former. Yet Burt concluded that whilst

'UK hydrodynamics research facilities and AWE's superior expertise' previously 'served to give the UK an advantage in this area of science ... this is probably no longer the case.'

The MDA and the NPT

In addition to highlighting the need for democratic accountability, Ainslie also argued that renewing the MDA would not be compatible with Britain's commitments under the Nuclear Non-Proliferation Treaty (NPT). The UK government's position was that 'movements under the MDA do not involve nuclear weapons or nuclear explosive devices'. However, Ainslie responded that such arrangements 'do involve key components of weapons'. For example, he pointed to how 'Sandia National Laboratory have said that they are supplying neutron generators for British Trident warheads. Tritium is filled with reservoirs for use in British warheads at the Savannah River Site.'

As such, Ainslie concluded that 'the transfer of the components and the exchange of design information are contrary to the principles of the NPT'. Furthermore, the high levels of government secrecy over the details of the agreement showed both the UK and the US's appreciation of the need to prevent discussion of this issue.

Concluding thoughts

In summary, the issues of legality, accountability and democracy highlighted by Ainslie regarding the MDA continue to apply to the debate over the Agreement today. It is therefore important to revisit the detailed research John Ainslie conducted—and reflect on its meaning for the UK—as it continues with its nuclear rearmament programme. In the lead up to the planned renewal of the MDA in 2024 the Nuclear Information Service will continue to advocate for Parliamentary scrutiny of the agreement.

Ainslie Archive

The Ainslie Archive is an ongoing project of the Nuclear Information Service to upload the vast archive of nuclear weapons researcher John Ainslie, who died in 2016.

You can already browse hundreds of documents, reports, press cuttings, de-classified UK, US and Russian government memos, dating back to the Cold War and the Cuban Missile Crisis, as well as more recent times.

Funding for this work has been received from Scottish CND, Lansbury House Trust and many individual donors.

Visit the archive at:

www.nuclearinfo.org/ainslie-archive

Nuclear dependency

Arguments from The Future of the British Bomb

John Ainslie

These excerpts are from The Future of the British Bomb *(2006), John Ainslie's comprehensive review of the issues raised by nuclear-armed Trident missiles carried on four British submarines. He begins by examining Britain's dependence on the United States for parts of Trident's warheads. The report was first published by the WMD Awareness Programme.*

The British Government acknowledges that Trident missiles are leased from the United States but claims that they carry British warheads. This description is questionable. The warhead is a copy of the US W76. A report by the Public Records Office refers to the Anglicisation of an American design. Several key components are produced in America. The warheads on Royal Navy Trident submarines could be more accurately described as Anglo-American rather than British.

The Neutron Generator is one vital part. It contributes to the initiation of nuclear fission. The MC2989 Neutron Generators initially deployed on British warheads were overhauled in the US in 1999. This implies that they were built there. A replacement Neutron Generator, MC4380, was manufactured in America and supplied to Britain in 2002. The Gas Reservoir in the warhead supplies tritium to boost the fission process. The reservoirs on British warheads are filled with tritium in the US. These are difficult components to build. This suggests that the reservoirs in British warheads are manufactured in America. The Arming, Fusing and Firing System triggers the warhead. The model used on British warheads was designed by Sandia Laboratory and almost certainly procured off-the-shelf from America.

The Trident system operated by Britain is not identical to that deployed by the US Navy, although it is very similar. One difference is the type of high explosive in the British warhead. US nuclear weapons laboratories are playing a critical role in assessing the long-term performance of this British explosive. A second difference is the Fire Control System. British submarines carry a slightly different model. But all the hardware and software for it is created in America. It is significant that, even where the British Trident system differs from the American version, US support is essential.

The US role in handling tritium and making the Neutron Generators is known from publicly available American sources. Yet when asked about these issues in Parliament the Defence Minister refused to answer, on grounds of national security. Successive governments have withheld information to conceal dependence. There is a deliberate attempt to create ambiguity over the extent of dependence. The true limitations of independence are concealed. This is consistent with the policy of uncertainty that lies at the heart of British nuclear policy.

Reliance on American support is not only of historical and current significance. It will remain a crucial factor so long as Britain remains a nuclear-weapons state. The terms of the Mutual Defence Agreement [between the United Kingdom and the United States] constrain how information and material that has been exchanged can be used. The British nuclear weapons establishment today is almost entirely dependent on this information. Any future nuclear programme will build on what exists today. It will be subject to the same limitations and must be in the mutual defence interest of both Britain and the United States.

A truly independent nuclear weapons programme is not an option. A future system might be more or less dependent on US support than at present. Current and future US Administrations will determine the degree of independence. Also, the US can probably restrict the independence of the system in service, should there be a change in policy in Washington.

Targeting systems

In 1988, the National Audit Office reported that it was essential that Trident targeting software be produced in Britain. As Trident entered service it was revealed that 'contractor support' had been required to complete this work. This contractor support almost certainly came from the United States.

Targeting data on British Trident submarines is processed in the Fire Control System by software produced in America. This data is created in the Nuclear Operations and Targeting Centre in London. The centre relies on US software. In 2002 the Fire Control Systems on British and American Trident submarines were modified. Just before this the computers in the London targeting centre were upgraded. The American applications used for target planning and for fire control are complex and unique. It would be possible for US programmers to modify the software supplied to Britain, either openly or covertly, to restrict how Trident could be used.

Even those who operate the system may not have an accurate perception of its dependence. The British Trident system is only as independent as Washington wants it to be. It could be argued that constraints on independence would be consistent with the Mutual Defence Agreement.

British warheads can be integrated into US attack plans. There are special arrangements for supplying US nuclear targeting information to Britain. The United Kingdom Liaison Cell at STRATCOM [Strategic Command] headquarters in Omaha plays a central role in this process. US support may also be required to produce plans for an independent attack.

The Nato Nuclear Planning System is a mechanism for preparing attacks by nuclear-armed aircraft. The crucial systems for targeting Britain's Trident force are bilateral. While there will be links between the British system and Nato headquarters, the essential networking is between London and the headquarters of STRATCOM. The instructions to order the use of British weapons are not issued in the form of Nato Emergency Action Messages, but through a unique system.

Trident missiles can only achieve the required level of accuracy if a special forecast of the weather over the target is available. This is supplied to British and American submarines in compressed messages transmitted every 12 hours by the US Navy. Trident also relies on gravity information from US sources. Without this weather and gravity data the missiles would be less accurate.

British Trident submarines are normally on a state of alert measured in days. There is a substantial American presence at the Northwood headquarters from where British submarine operations are controlled. If the alert state of British Trident were raised, the US would almost certainly know. This would give them several days' notice of any British nuclear attack.

Communications with British Trident submarines can be made through British or Nato systems. In addition there are bilateral systems. These are likely to be used for key data. Submarines can receive messages on a wide range of frequencies. In future it will be possible to use Extremely High Frequency (EHF), but only through a transmitter on an American satellite. EHF is important because it is considered to be less vulnerable than other systems during a nuclear war.

* * *

The effects of nuclear use

A single Trident warhead used against a military installation, such as a naval base in Northern Russia, could cause around 23,000 civilian fatalities. If the target was inside a city then there could be 150,000 –

200,000 deaths. If the warheads from one British submarine were exploded at military targets in the Moscow area, most of them outside the city, this could result in around 3 million deaths. This figure would rise to between 9 and 30 million if the warheads on all three armed submarines were detonated. These figures only include short-term fatalities. The long-term effects of radiation, environmental damage and the destruction of infrastructure would substantially increase the death rate. Studies have shown that a US counterforce attack on strategic military targets in Russia would result in massive civilian casualties. The raw figures do not give a true picture of the horror that would be inflicted on individual women, men and children. The photographs and accounts from Hiroshima and Nagasaki provide a glimpse of the monstrosity of nuclear weapons.

Accident

A US study distinguishes three types of nuclear accident scenario. The first situation is an unauthorised launch of a weapon by a rogue commander or a terrorist. The second is where a launch takes places by mistake, as a result of a training accident or a system malfunction. The third scenario is where incorrect information results in an intentional launch.

A number of situations fall into this third category. There could be an error or malfunction in the early-warning systems which are designed to detect a missile attack. A non-threatening event could be misinterpreted. There could be a false perception that another country had launched a nuclear attack, or a misperception that a nuclear weapon had detonated within the homeland. Lastly, a training attack could be misinterpreted as a real attack.

The report touches on the connections between the possession of nuclear weapons, relations between Russia and the US, and the risk of accidental use. It suggests that de-alerting moves could improve relations between the two countries and so provide a basis for more substantial measures. It recommends that several immediate unilateral measures be taken within 6 to 12 months. One proposal is to move Trident submarines further from Russia. Britain's Trident force is not mentioned, but for geographical reasons it could be seen as a particular threat because of the proximity of patrol areas to Russia.

The analysis concludes, 'The risk of accidental or unauthorised nuclear use is too high given the markedly improved relationship between the United States and Russia. This is in part because nuclear weapons now play a role out of proportion to other aspects of the relationship'. Adherence to nuclear deterrence is an obstacle to progress towards lowering risks and improving relations – 'A central reason for the phased approach is that some options for improving safety would push too far beyond current deterrence practices and orthodoxies to be acceptable'.

The risk of a nuclear weapons accident has been considered particularly in the context of the large American and Russian arsenals on a high state of alert. But the dangers also apply to other nuclear powers. For Britain's part there is a need to recognise that our nuclear weapons contribute to the risk of an accident. Also each step that we take towards disarmament will contribute to building a better relationship with Russia. What is blocking progress is continued adherence to outdated and dangerous theories about nuclear deterrence.

Financial costs

Cost will be a major factor determining the future of British nuclear weapons. Michael Quinlan [civil servant] concedes that if today he had to decide whether or not to embark on the Trident programme then the cost would not be justified. Admiral Sir Raymond Lygo suggested that the cost of Trident should be capped at a level relative to the threat from Russia and China.

The substantial overheads of the nuclear-powered submarine programme are partly due to Trident and partly to the conventionally-armed force. The primary mission of the latter is the protection of Trident. There are huge potential savings to be made by giving up nuclear-powered submarines. Estimates of the cost of decommissioning defence nuclear facilities have increased several times in recent years. The long-term costs of storing nuclear waste will increase with each year Britain continues to have nuclear weapons and nuclear-powered submarines.

In assessing the cost of upgrading Trident, or acquiring a replacement, the budget should include not only capital costs but also the total revenue cost throughout the planned life of the system, including decommissioning.

***

John Ainslie sent this additional paper to the Defence Select Committee in 2007 after he gave evidence to their inquiry on nuclear weapons. It develops some of the issues raised in The Future of the British Bomb.

Is Trident Crippled?

In 1988, an Audit Office report into the Trident programme said:

> 'proving the effectiveness of the system for UK purposes is dependent on the

production in the UK of software for targeting, modelling and effectiveness assessment'.

The report pointed out that at the time the Director General Strategic Weapon Systems was having difficulty recruiting suitable staff. In 1994, the Defence Minister said that software development work had been completed using a mix of internal expertise and specialist contractor support.

Reliance on US software

The designers of the Trident D5 adopted a systems-wide approach to meet the accuracy specifications of the missile. They studied and modelled each factor that could reduce accuracy and created a substantial complex of software, computer models and data. These are not static but are regularly updated. While the United Kingdom does produce some software for the British Trident system, much of it is of US origin.

The Applied Physics Laboratory of Johns Hopkins University in Maryland (APL) evaluates the UK Trident missile system. APL designed the systems used to monitor missile tests and they analyse all British tests. Additional analysis is carried out by Charles Stark Draper Laboratories, who make the missile guidance system.

The Trident Fire Control hardware is manufactured by General Dynamics Defense Systems (GDDS). The US Navy regularly places contracts with GDDS for updates of software for the UK fire control system.

K Department of the Naval Surface Warfare Center at Dahlgren in Virginia develops and tests the targeting and fire control software for Trident. The contractor who supports K Department is required to – 'coordinate the development of fire control specifications for the United States and United Kingdom submarine-launched ballistic missile (SLBM) systems and support specification testing ... perform the verification, acceptance, static and/or dynamic testing tasks for up models including Fire Control support software, United Kingdom reference/simulation models, US/UK targeting models and SLBM general purpose tools'.

The models referred to are at the heart of the Trident system. They are used for shore-based targeting and performance assessment. In addition parts of these models are integrated into the fire control software on Trident submarines.

In the British software facility programmers maintain, update and modify US codes and models for inclusion in the suite of codes for the UK Trident system.

Validation of US software in the United Kingdom
When asked about the verification of US fire control software, Defence Minister Des Browne said,

> 'Each new release of Trident fire control software is certified by the US Government under the terms of the Polaris Sales Agreement (as amended for Trident). Under the agreement, the UK has the capability to validate the software models for software performance and verify that the findings are correct. This is undertaken and independently verified by UK experts to ensure the software meets our requirements before being issued to Royal Navy submarines.'

Adam Ingram, junior Defence Minister, was asked about US software for the shore-based system and said,

> 'The UK shore-based target planning system for Trident is validated through a range of UK and US research programmes. UK experts then independently verify the system against requirements before issuing it to Royal Navy submarines'.

Work on software for Trident is carried out in the Corsham Computer Centre also referred to as the Corsham Software Facility. This is an underground complex close to Basil Hill Barracks in Wiltshire. Mass Consultants Ltd manage the IT system in the centre, on behalf of the Strategic Systems Integrated Project Team. Analysts who assess the performance and effectiveness of Trident use the IT facilities in centre.

The one company in the United Kingdom with expertise in analysing submarine-launched ballistic missile trajectories was Hunting Engineering Ltd. The company changed its name to INSYS and then to Lockheed Martin UK. They now are a subsidiary of the US firm with the main Trident contract. Some of the validation will be carried out at Corsham but other work is probably contracted out to Lockheed Martin UK.

Removal of classified items from US software
British experts will be hampered in their attempt to validate the software by the constraints of US security restrictions. The Joint Strike Fighter deal showed the difficulties of purchasing equipment which is dependent on sensitive American software. In the case of Trident the United States does supply the software codes, but not in their original complete form.

A substantial proportion of US nuclear targeting information is classified so that only US citizens can see it. The Chief of Staff has issued a directive specifying how classified items should be removed from nuclear targeting information, in a process called sanitising, before it is handed to the Corsham Computer Centre, the London targeting centre or the British contingent at Strategic Command in Omaha. The contractor at Dahlgren has to check that any software handed to Britain has been sanitized, as part of the Quality Assurance (QA) process –

'For the QA of UK models, the contractor shall analyse the software, data and documentation to verify that all US-only items have been removed.'

This implies that the process is as follows:
1. US contractors produce software items for the US Trident system
2. US-only items are removed from the code, data tables and instruction manuals
3. A US contractor verifies that these items have all been removed
4. The cut-down software is handed to the Corsham Computer Centre
5. Corsham and Lockheed Martin UK check that the software works
6. The software is issued to submarines, the London Targeting Centre and/or the Corsham Computer Centre as appropriate.

Implications for the independence of UK Trident
From the perspective of Washington it would be desirable to create the impression that Britain can use Trident independently while at the same time maintaining a veto over actual use. One particular concern will be the potential for Britain to launch 144 nuclear warheads at the United States. How could the software stop a Trident launch?

General restrictions
Preventing the use in all circumstances except tests, or preventing the missiles from being fired westwards, towards the United States from the normal patrol areas, should be possible.

Restricting the system to only NATO or joint US/UK plans
The fire control system can probably distinguish an independent British plan from a NATO or Anglo-American plan. Any allied or joint plan would have to be deconflicted. This is a process of integrating two plans to ensure that they do not undermine each other's effectiveness. For example debris in the fallout cloud from the explosion of a British nuclear explosion could cripple a US nuclear weapon and prevent it from

detonating. For reasons of complexity and classification it is not possible to run a US attack plan through the British computer system. Deconflicting can only be carried out by running the British plan through the main US nuclear planning system at Strategic Command in Omaha. This deconflicting process is likely to leave a trace in the data which could be detected by the fire control software on the submarine. If the software can distinguish a Nato plan from an independent one, then it could possibly prevent the independent plan from being implemented.

Restricting use by manipulating weather data
A NATO or Anglo-American plan would probably use US weather data. The fire control system requires details of weather over the target area if it is to achieve the desired level of accuracy. For an attack on Russia a large amount of data is required on wind speed and air density at various altitudes. This data has to be transmitted over very low frequency (VLF). It is compressed and formatted in the US into Ballistic Parameters (Balpars). These are transmitted every 12 hours. There are similar mechanisms for producing detailed weather data when Trident is being re-targeted against specific targets. It is possible that information could be contained within Balpars or other weather data that would have the effect of switching on or off the UK fire control system.

If the US tampered with the software, would we find out? The US Navy asked Mountain State Information Systems to check the security of the US Trident software. The company's description of this work reveals that this was a complex task for which they had to develop new techniques. This suggests that if the US programmers tried to hide commands within the software it would not be easy for British experts to find them.

The task is made particularly difficult because of the holes in the code, data and manuals where items have been removed for reasons of security. This means that there will be parts of the UK software which do not make sense. But the US manufacturers will not be able to explain the anomalies because the missing material is classified.

As the software has a mixture of cut-down US components and British elements it will be a difficult task to get it to work. This is probably the main focus of the British software effort. Checking to see if the Americans have crippled the code is probably not a priority.

This does not establish that the software has been crippled, but does suggest that it could be. The only way that Britain can guarantee that the Trident software has not been modified would be to produce it all ourselves. But we do not currently have the expertise to do this.

Trident: Nowhere to Go

John Ainslie

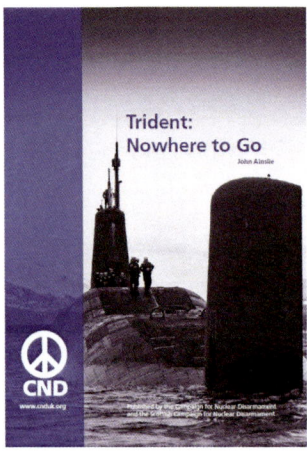

Trident: Nowhere to Go *was published in February 2012 by CND and Scottish CND, shortly after the* Your Scotland, Your Referendum *consultation opened.*

Summary

Officials in the Ministry of Defence (MOD) have told the *Financial Times* that they are looking at the consequences of Scottish independence for the Trident programme. Key questions are whether the nuclear fleet could be moved, and if so where? Defence Secretary Philip Hammond said that relocating Trident would cost billions and take many years.[1] Admiral Lord West added that moving the nuclear armaments depot from Coulport would be a "huge, huge complex operation".[2]

Almost 50 years ago the MOD drew up a list of possible locations for Polaris, including sites in England and Wales. Today these papers will be dusted off. Officials may also revive an option that was raised in 1981: basing the UK Trident fleet in the United States. A second overseas possibility would be Ile Longue in France. Building a floating support ship would be a further option.

This report examines the feasibility of these alternatives. There are major obstacles to each one of them. A government which had deep pockets and which placed nuclear weapons at the top of their agenda could, with enough political will and financial commitment, find some way to relocate Trident. However, the economic and political realities of today mean that none of the alternatives are practical.

There were three English sites on the Polaris shortlist. One was Portland, near Weymouth. Part of the area which would be required for Trident has been transformed into the sailing venue for the 2012 Olympics. David Cameron is keen to stress the legacy that the Olympics will leave, but even he would find it difficult to argue that this should mean parking nuclear-armed submarines at Weymouth.

A second alternative was Devonport. The MOD considered transforming the Cornish shore, opposite the dockyard, into a nuclear weapons' store. To accommodate Trident they would have to buy Antony House and its grounds from the National Trust. In addition to the great difficulty of acquiring this site, the nuclear depot would be too close to a residential estate. The Office of Nuclear Regulation would almost certainly try to block any proposal to build a nuclear missile store next to a city with a population of a quarter of a million.

The third location was Falmouth. The proposed submarine base would be on National Trust land close to St Just in Roseland. Acquiring this would be very difficult if not impossible. The warhead depot would be North of Falmouth. Two villages would be so close to the depot that they would have to be abandoned. Both are significant centres for watersports, especially Mylor in Churchtown. In 1963 the MOD concluded that the costs of acquiring and developing this site for Polaris would be so great that the project wasn't feasible. A Trident depot would be much larger and even less viable. Jobs that might arise from introducing Trident would be offset by a major decline in the watersports industry and tourism.

In 1963 officials proposed combining a submarine base at Devonport with an armaments depot at Falmouth. But there would still be huge problems at the two sites. This plan would still mean introducing nuclear missiles into Plymouth and taking over a large peninsula on the Fal estuary. A nuclear missile depot would ruin the tourism and watersports industries in Falmouth and bring few long-term jobs.

An existing nuclear site that could be considered is Barrow in Furness, where the submarines are built. This might be suitable if the Navy only deploy Trident when there is a full moon and a high tide. Otherwise it is a non-starter. Walney Channel is too shallow for a submarine base. The Barrow option falls at the first hurdle and was not seriously considered in 1963.

The one Welsh location on the old shortlist was Milford Haven. Siting Polaris here would have resulted in the closure of one oil refinery. Introducing Trident in this estuary today would end three major petrochemical facilities and cut off one of Britain's main sources of gas. The grounds for dismissing Milford Haven, as with all the other sites, are even stronger today than they were fifty years ago.

In 1963 each of these options was rejected. In 1979 Sir Frank Cooper, Permanent Under Secretary at the MOD, went further. He said it was most unlikely that they could build a replacement for Coulport on any greenfield site.[3] After the end of the Cold War and with growing awareness of environmental issues, the objections to such a development would be louder and more wide-ranging.

In 1981 the MOD seriously considered "US basing" of the British Trident fleet, including nuclear warheads, to avoid the cost of expanding Coulport. However, they soon found that this ploy was fraught with problems. To comply with the Non Proliferation Treaty they would have to build unique British facilities in America, rather than use the US Navy ones. The force would also be transparently even less independent than it already was.

Rather than bumping into each other in the night, British and French nuclear submarine fleets could come together and share one base in Brittany. But Ile Longue is far too small to allow room for the separate British facilities that would be required. As with the American option, Britain would have to find a greenfield site somewhere else in Brittany to turn into a nuclear base. The political problems would almost certainly be insurmountable.

At various points in the 1960s and 1970s Britain considered following the American example and acquiring a support ship which could be a floating Polaris submarine depot.

Implementing this today with Trident would only be possible if the MOD reverted to a 1960s approach to nuclear safety and persuaded the US Government to endorse this step back in time.

Scotland shouldn't be expected to keep Trident just because no-one else will have it. Admiral Lord West suggested that independence for Scotland would result in unilateral nuclear disarmament.[4] This is something which many people in Scotland, England, Wales and the rest the world would welcome. Those who call for a nuclear-weapons-free Scotland cannot be accused of taking a "Not In My Back Yard" approach. Removing Trident from Scotland would mean there were no nuclear weapons in Britain. This could give a new push to global efforts towards a nuclear-weapons-free world. There is now a huge question mark over the future of the British nuclear weapons programme.

Options in England and Wales

General Points

An account of how the MOD assessed where to base the Polaris force is given by Malcolm Chalmers and William Walker in *Uncharted Waters: the UK, nuclear weapons and the Scottish question*.[5]

There are two components of any nuclear-armed submarine base. One is a site to berth and support the submarines. The second is a depot to store and handle nuclear warheads and missiles. There are particular problems with finding a suitable site for the latter.

Nuclear armaments depot

When the MOD were considering where to put Polaris their requirement was that the armaments depot should be 4,400 feet (1.34 kilometres) from any significant area of housing and one mile (1.6 kilometres) from the submarine base.[6] The Polaris depot at Coulport, built on this basis, occupied an area of 128 hectares.[7]

By 1979 the safety criteria had changed:

> "The rules for establishing protection from explosives by laying down 'quality distances' from such explosives – whether in magazines or process buildings – to inhabited buildings and public roads, were changed after the Coulport complex was constructed. As a result, waivers have had to be granted to enable some of the existing buildings to be used."[8]

This suggests that the old Polaris area in Coulport was not sufficiently far from inhabited buildings and public roads to comply with the criteria which applied in the 1970s.

In 1979, as the MOD looked at the implications of acquiring Trident, they realised that there would be two major problems at Coulport. Firstly, the new missiles would have more explosive power than Polaris and so they could not use the existing facilities. Secondly, the new bunkers would have to comply with the new safety criteria which required greater separation from residential properties.

The issue was considered by officials at the top of the MOD. Richard Mottram, Private Secretary to the Permanent Under Secretary, pointed out that this was "one of the most difficult technical areas which we need to explore."[9] Michael Quinlan, Deputy Under Secretary (Policy), said "we would face complex and perhaps very serious problems over accommodating it at Coulport with present explosives regulations".[10] The MOD drew up a plan to expand Coulport to 1067 hectares, eight times its original size.[11] Under this proposal they would have been maintaining as well as storing missiles, as had been the case with Polaris.

At that time Mrs Thatcher's government had been intending to buy the Trident C4 missile. In 1982 they opted to purchase the much larger D5 missile instead. The problems with Coulport became far greater. As a result the government decided to transfer the missile maintenance work to the United States.[12] There was still a requirement to handle and store D5 missiles and their nuclear warheads at the Loch Long depot. Even though Coulport would no longer be overhauling missiles, the depot still had to be expanded to three times its original size. The site is 2.9 kilometres from East to West and 2.1 kilometres from North to South.

The explosive safety criteria meant that the buildings had to be separate from each other and far from public areas. The Explosives Handling Jetty at Coulport, which loads and unloads missiles and warheads from submarines, is 800 metres from other facilities. Within the high-security Trident Special Area there are three compounds – Ready Issue Magazines for missiles, nuclear-warhead storage magazines and a nuclear-warhead processing building. These three facilities are each 400 metres apart. The Ready Issues Magazines are a series of bunkers, each of which can take one Trident missile. The bunkers are 27 metres apart to reduce the risk that the detonation of one missile would result in the explosion of others.

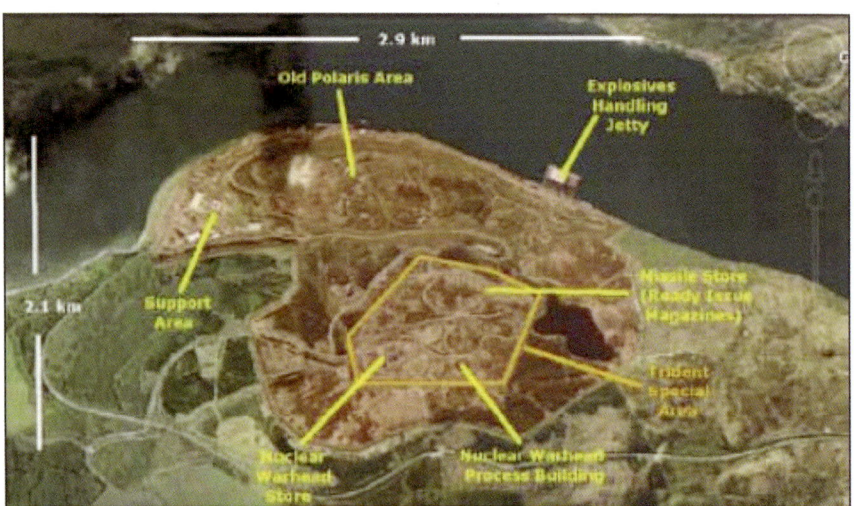

▲ Trident nuclear missile and warhead depot Coulport

Most of the logistical and support facilities in Coulport are more than 1 kilometre from the Trident Special Area and the Explosives Handling Jetty. In addition to the large area of the base itself there is a wider zone around it within which there are very few residential buildings.

There are similar separation distances, between facilities and from public areas, at the American Trident bases at King's Bay in Georgia and Bangor in Washington State.

The US Navy is building a new Explosives Handling Jetty for Trident at the Bangor base. Anti-nuclear campaigner Glen Milner has been trying for seven years to obtain information on the explosives' safety distances associated with this development. Despite a ruling from the Supreme Court in Milner's favour, the Department of Defense have still not released the data. They are currently trying to introduce legislation in Congress to block the disclosure. The British government are unlikely to be any more open about how they would calculate the safety zones for a new Trident facility.

The MOD's risk assessment for an accident involving an armed Trident submarine in the Faslane shiplift assumes that the detonation of one missile would result in the explosion of all the missiles on a submarine and the dispersal of plutonium from all the nuclear warheads onboard.[13] Consequently at any site where there is a fully-armed submarine there is the risk, not just of the detonation of a single missile, but of all the missiles on the vessel. The rocket fuel on a Trident D5 missile is equivalent to over 70 tonnes of TNT.[14]

When the reductions announced in the Strategic Defence and Security Review are implemented, each submarine will carry 8 missiles, ie around 560 tonnes of TNT equivalent in rocket fuel. The risk of a missile explosion is highest at the Explosives Handling Jetty. The nuclear warheads are located in a circle around the third stage of the D5 missile. This third stage could detonate in the event of an impact. This fundamental weakness in the D5 design is well known. Current British practice is to load and unload warheads from the missiles while they are in the submarine, rather than to unload armed missiles and then separate the warheads on shore. However the removal of armed missiles is not ruled out.

▲ Coulport - Ready Issue Magazines

▲ Coulport - Reentry Body Magazines

In reviewing their long-term plans for nuclear weapons, the MOD assume that safety regulations may be tighter in future than they are today. So the safety distances which were applied in the design of the Trident area at Coulport are likely to be a minimum. Spacing between facilities and separation from built-up areas would probably have to be greater than at

Coulport. Reductions in missile numbers might mean that the number of Ready Issue Magazines was reduced from 16 to 8. The smaller nuclear warhead stockpile might be incorporated in one magazine building rather than the two at Coulport. However, these reductions are unlikely to have a significant effect on the overall size of the area required for a depot, and would be offset by increasing spacing distances.

The Coulport depot today takes up an area of 364 hectares. It has 32 kilometres of internal roads and 30 kilometres of alarmed fence.[15] Allowing for the fact that the present site includes the old Polaris Special Area, a new depot would probably require around 300 hectares. This is equivalent to an area of 1.5 kilometres by 2 kilometres.

When revisiting the alternative locations considered in 1963 it is important to bear in mind that a Trident depot would be more than twice the size of the Polaris depot that was originally envisaged, and separation distances from inhabited areas would be greater.

Submarine base

Safety is a consideration in the siting of the submarine base as well as the armaments depot. A support base would have a shiplift or drydock for submarine maintenance. Current practice is to lift fully-armed Trident submarines in the Faslane shiplift. This introduces substantial risks. In addition Power Range Testing of reactors is carried out at the berths. A Trident submarine presents a particularly complex cocktail of risks. It combines high-explosive rocket fuel, nuclear warheads, torpedoes and a nuclear power plant. The MOD's risk assessments acknowledge the possibility that a missile accident could result in a release of radioactive material from the reactor.

1963 Polaris assessment

The MOD considered five factors: (1) Ease of submarine operations; (2) Safety; (3) Logistics; (4) Ownership, development costs and planning permission; and (5) Overall cost. Chalmers and Walker suggest that a sixth factor should be introduced – the political risk at local, national and international level of pursuing particular options.[16]

Sites on the East coast of England were ruled out because they were too far from the deep water of the Atlantic where submarines could avoid detection. The effect of this was to focus on the Celtic fringe – Scotland, Wales and Cornwall. Harland and Wolfe shipyard in Belfast was considered but it was not a serious contender. For political as well as practical reasons it would not be pursued today. Sites on islands or remote locations were eliminated in 1963 because providing logistical support would be difficult.

After an initial wide review of options, the study shortlisted 10 sites for detailed consideration. Six of these were in Scotland. There was one site in Wales (Milford Haven) and three in England (Devonport, Falmouth and Portland).

Greenfield sites

It is highly questionable whether the MOD could successfully introduce nuclear weapons and nuclear submarines to a new site. In 1979, when drawing up their plans for Trident, the MOD had doubts about whether Coulport could be adapted for the new missile system.[17] Michael Quinlan said "A new 'greenfield' site in the UK should I suggest, be assumed as a last (but not impossible) recourse."[18] Frank Cooper, Permanent Secretary at the MOD, replied that "while nothing is impossible, it is most unlikely that we would ever get agreement to a new 'greenfield' site in the UK".[19] He added that the MOD should not delude themselves into thinking that a greenfield site was acceptable.[20]

Devonport

At first glance, the most obvious alternative for Trident would be Devonport. Refits of Trident submarines are carried out in Devonport yard and conventionally-armed nuclear-powered submarines are based here, although the last of them are due to depart in 2017.

Moving Trident to Devonport would mean finding space for the submarines within the existing site and finding somewhere to build a nuclear armaments depot. In 1963 the proposal was to build the depot on the Cornish side of the Tamar at Wilcove.[21] There was concern about the response from the National Trust, who own Antony House. The Polaris plan would have come close to this historic property. The Trident proposal, needing twice as much land, would completely swallow up Antony House and its grounds. It would only be viable if the National Trust sold the building and its extensive gardens to the MOD. Antony House was the setting for Tim Burton's recent film *Alice in Wonderland* in which Johnny Depp played the Mad Hatter.[22]

A second problem that was foreseen in the 1960s was the proximity of the MOD Thanckes Oil Depot. If a large Trident facility was built at Wilcove then the oil depot would have to close. The MOD would be forced to find an alternative location where they could build a fuel depot for the ships at Devonport.

The MOD was concerned that their proposed Polaris depot would have been too close to the village of Wilcove. A larger Trident depot would certainly take over the village, which would have to be abandoned. There would be further problems with the housing estate near HMS Raleigh, as this would be immediately next to the nuclear depot. Even the old 1960s criteria of maintaining a gap of 1.34 kilometres from any residential housing could not be met.

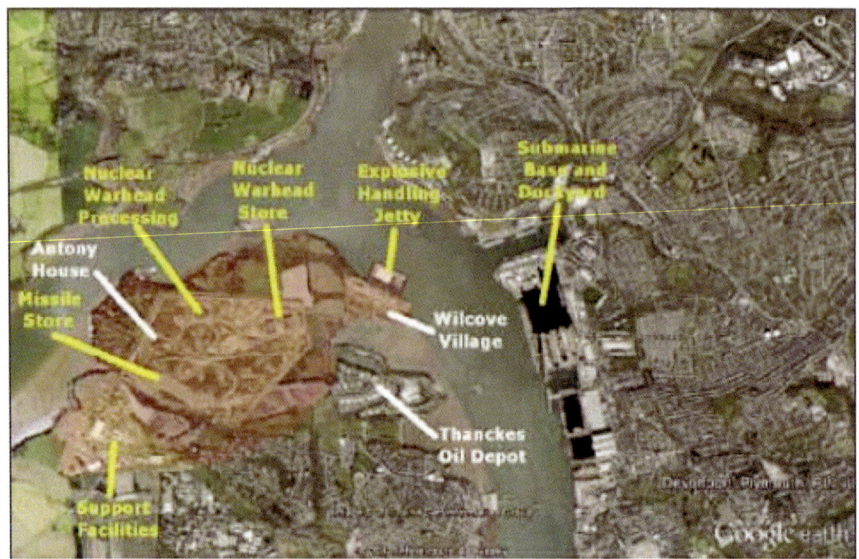

▲ Areas required for a nuclear armaments depot and Trident submarine base at Devonport

A damning factor is that Devonport is in the city of Plymouth which has a population of 250,000. The Nuclear Installations Inspectorate and their successors, the Office of Nuclear Regulation (ONR), have approved the development and continued use of nuclear refuelling facilities at Devonport. However, they are aware that the siting of this nuclear facility in a major urban area is contrary to normal practice. It is inconceivable that the ONR would approve the construction of a new nuclear missile depot so close to a city.

Falmouth

The 1963 proposal was to build a nuclear armaments depot near Penarrow Point and a submarine base on the opposite side of the estuary between St Just in Roseland and St Mawes.[23] The photo superimposes images of Faslane and Coulport on these two sites to indicate what a nuclear base at Falmouth would look like.

Whereas the Polaris proposal would have taken up the land around

Penarrow Point, a Trident armaments depot would swallow up the whole peninsular, including the villages of Mylor Churchtown in the North and Flushing in the South. The depot would also extend to the West, towards Penryn and Mylor Bridge.

The depth of the Fal estuary restricts where it would be possible to build the Explosives Handling Jetty and submarine berths. There is deep channel which zig-zags across the estuary.[24] The key facilities could only be sited where this channel is close to the shore, South of Penarrow Point on the Western shore and near St Just in Roseland on the Eastern shore. Other parts of the shoreline are too shallow for nuclear submarines.

▲ Areas required for a nuclear armaments depot and Trident submarine base at Falmouth

The site of the Explosives Handling Jetty (EHJ) would be 800 metres South East of Mylor Churchtown. The missile or warheads buildings would be a similar distance from the village. Mylor Churchtown is a significant sailing centre with 400 pleasure craft at the marina and nearby moorings. It is home to Restronguet Sailing Club, where the triple-Olympic Gold medallist Ben Ainslie learned to sail. The EHJ and bunkers would be so close that the village and surrounding area would have to be evacuated. The marina, sailing club and moorings would all be abandoned. Many of the houses on the road between Mylor Churchtown and Mylor

Bridge could no longer be inhabited. People living in Flushing would also have to leave their homes as they would be too close to the nuclear bunkers. The peninsula is between 1.4 kilometres and 2 kilometres in width. Wherever the nuclear facilities were placed on the peninsula, they would be too close to both Mylor Churchtown and Flushing.

At Coulport there is a Restricted Area of water 700 metres from the shore in Loch Long. There is a further Protected Area within 250 metres of the shore. Pleasure craft which sail close to the nuclear depot are intercepted by MOD Police patrol boats and warned to keep clear. There are no yachts or dinghies moored off Coulport.

▲ Mylor Churchtown

▲ Explosives Handling Jetty (Coulport)

If a similar zone was imposed around a nuclear depot in the Fal estuary then it could affect 581 moorings in Falmouth Harbour. The moorings would be on the perimeter of a high-security nuclear-weapons facility and many would have to be abandoned. The owners would find it very difficult to find alternatives places for their vessels. There is a five year waiting list for moorings around Falmouth. In addition, a large number of boats are stored on shore in Ganges Close, Mylor Churchtown. This area would be near the centre of the nuclear weapons store and no longer available as a dinghy park. A large number of moorings at St Just in Roseland might also have to be abandoned due to their proximity to the shiplift and jetties.

The population of Falmouth, around 20,000, is similar to Helensburgh, the nearest town to Faslane. However, whereas Helensburgh is 7.4 kilometres from the Faslane shiplift and 8 kilometres from Coulport, Falmouth would be 500 metres from the boundary of the depot and 1.5 kilometres from the missile and nuclear warhead buildings.

In addition to the explosives safety zone, there would be a wider area within which there would be preplanned countermeasures for a nuclear accident. This would extend to 2 kilometres from the nuclear facilities in the depot and would include a large part of Falmouth.

Falmouth has its employment problems, but Trident would not provide the answer. Tourism, particularly watersports, is a major part of the local economy. The loss of 1,000 pleasure craft would be a significant blow to the area, complemented by the tourism blight of a nuclear weapons base.

The 1963 proposal for the submarine base was to build it on the Eastern shore of the estuary, North of St Mawes, with a floating dry-dock close to St Just in Roseland. This section of coast is owned by the National Trust, as part of their effort to protect the British coastline, particularly in Cornwall. Officials in the MOD assumed that the National Trust would object to their proposals for Polaris and that there would be public backing for the Trust's stance. This was a major factor in their elimination of the Falmouth option.

The MOD thought that developing the armaments depot would be very expensive. One factor was the difficulty in adapting the terrain. Another was the considerable cost and complication of land purchase.

They were concerned that both the National Trust and the Duchy of Cornwall might block their proposal. In addition to its land holdings, the Duchy owns all the foreshore in the county. Prince Charles might find himself torn between his affinity with the Royal Navy and his promotion of produce from the pristine environment of Cornwall.

Devonport and Falmouth

Faced with the difficulty of finding a suitable site for a nuclear ammunitions depot in Devonport, the 1963 review considered the possibility of combining Devonport and Falmouth. Devonport could house the submarine base and Falmouth the nuclear weapon store. The MOD rejected this arrangement because it would "stretch to an unacceptable degree the requirement for proximity of the operating base and the RNAD".[25] They insisted that the ammunitions depot should be within one hour's sailing of the submarine base. Falmouth is 70 kilometres West of Devonport.

Chalmers and Walker suggest that with the lower tempo of nuclear submarine operations today, splitting the facilities between these two sites might be more acceptable than it was in 1963. This raises the issue of keeping submarines on patrol. There is a strong argument that Britain should, at the very least, end its Cold War posture of having one Trident submarine on patrol at all times. However, the submarine service is resisting this move. They fear that the rational for Trident will unravel if continuous patrols are ended.

This two-base option was supported by Dr Jeremy Stocker, a Commander in the Royal Navy and associate fellow at the Royal United

Services Institute, in his evidence to the House of Commons Defence Committee in 2006: "If the [nuclear deterrent] had to be relocated, the only viable base is Devonport, with a new RN Armament Depot probably at Falmouth."[26]

The Devonport-Falmouth option would get round the problem of acquiring land at St Just in Roseland or Wilcove from the National Trust. However, the problems of proximity to urban areas at both sites would remain. Introducing submarines armed with missile and nuclear warheads would significantly increase the risks of an explosive/nuclear accident in Plymouth. The armaments depot would still be too close to the town of Falmouth and would have a dramatic effect on the surrounding area.

Separating the facilities would change the proposal that would be presented to Falmouth. If only the warheads and missiles are based on the estuary then the area would be faced with the limitations and blight of hosting nuclear weapons, together with the loss of a large area of land, without the jobs associated with a submarine base. There would be short-term jobs building the depot, but most of the long-term posts would go to Devonport. The positions available at the nuclear missile depot would be mostly security jobs – as armed police telling visitors that they can't go along their favoured walk or sail too close to the shore.

[Analysis of issues related to Portland (Weymouth), Milford Haven, Barrow and overseas options is available in the original report]

Trident and Scottish independence

If Scotland was independent and insisted on the removal of nuclear weapons, then what would happen?

Philip Hammond said that Scotland would be forced to pay towards the costs of relocating Trident.[27] Admiral West adopted a similar line saying, "If this was forced on us by separation, then a lot of the costs for clean-up, for want of a better word, should be carried by Scotland."[28] Lord Robertson added: "If the SNP dogmatically demand the withdrawal of Trident it will have to pay multibillion-pound compensation for it to be relocated".[29]

But these are idle threats. Following the collapse of the Soviet Union, the Ukraine, Belarus and Kazakhstan found themselves as independent countries with large numbers of nuclear weapons. It is ridiculous to suggest that these three countries should each have paid Russia to build new nuclear missile silos.

The Black Sea Fleet was divided between Russia and Ukraine. Russia paid Ukraine to retain more than half of the ships.[30] Part of the agreement was that all nuclear weapons would be removed from the fleet. The Russian Navy withdrew its nuclear-armed submarines from their base at Balaclava, scene of the Thin Red Line in the Crimean War. This massive underground complex is now a tourist attraction.[31]

The second reason why Hammond's threats are hollow is that relocation is not a serious option. The MOD are beginning to realise that if an independent Scotland holds its ground on Trident, then Britain would have to abandon its nuclear weapons programme. Just one week after the Defence Minister said Scotland would bear the costs of a new base, MOD officials were presenting a very different line. They explained that Scottish independence would be the "nightmare scenario" for Trident and that London would pay any price to keep Faslane and Coulport.[32]

If the appearance of an independent anti-nuclear Scotland was imminent, then the London government would remove all nuclear weapons from Scotland prior to independence. Washington would insist that the American-built missiles and the nuclear warheads, which contain American components, were removed from Faslane and Coulport.

Warhead storage and processing facilities at Burghfield can only handle a limited number of warheads. When Chevaline was withdrawn from service many of the warheads were taken from Coulport to RAF Honington rather than Burghfield. They were stored there until they were due for dismantling. Faced with an independent anti-nuclear Scotland the MOD would move the existing stockpile of Trident warheads to Honington for temporary storage. Trident missiles would be returned to Kings Bay in America.

Some commentators suggest the UK might force an independent Scotland to continue to host nuclear weapons. However, this assumes that there is solid support for Trident in the London establishment. Historically there has always been an element of questioning, within Whitehall, of Britain retaining nuclear weapons, particularly from the Treasury. This is likely to be a significant force today with an economic crisis and expensive plans for Trident replacement. Since the end of the Cold War the rationale for British nuclear weapons has become significantly weaker. There is a reluctance to express the gut feeling that Britain needs nuclear weapons to be great, because this is contrary to our image as a responsible power concerned about proliferation.

There is a pro-Trident lobby within the UK defence establishment, but it is not all powerful. Trident is competing with other defence programmes – not just with spending on the Army and Air Force, but also on surface ships in the Navy.

It is wrong to assume that the US government's approach to Scottish independence will be based the issue of nuclear weapons. Successive US governments have supported the UK nuclear programme, but their enthusiasm for doing so should not be exaggerated. There is no example of a British Prime Minister going to an American President and asking to get out of the nuclear business. The nearest case was when Harold Wilson was first elected Prime Minister. The US State Department thought Wilson was going to abandon nuclear weapons, so they prepared a briefing for President Johnson setting out how America could help him to carry out his disarmament policy. When they met, Wilson told Johnston that he wasn't in favour of disarmament, so the State department's briefing notes were superfluous.

In 1981 the British Embassy in Washington told the MOD that although Jimmy Carter had signed off the initial Trident deal, he had not been enthusiastic –

"the 1980 agreement was concluded only after serious doubts on the part of President Carter himself had, with considerable difficulty, been overcome".[33]

They added that although President Reagan, who was in post at the time, was fully supportive –

"It would be unwise to assume that future US Administrations will necessarily take quite so positive an attitude."[34]

Today the Obama administration's approach to nuclear weapons is dominated by other concerns. Support for the British programme may be a peripheral issue.

In the past the US-UK nuclear relationship has been kept firmly under the control of a very small number of individuals who are committed to supporting the British programme. The State Department in Washington is deliberately kept on the margins. Faced with the complex political issue of Scottish independence, this may change.

There is a long history of support for nuclear disarmament in Scotland. The first Polaris submarines to arrive in Britain were American vessels sent to the Holy Loch in 1961. The imposition of these Weapons of Mass Destruction on the Clyde sparked nationwide opposition. Key institutions in civic Scotland, such as the churches and trade unions, have maintained solid resistance to Polaris and Trident over recent decades.

The different perpectives North and South of the border can be seen by comparing debates on nuclear weapons in Westminster and Holyrood. In London a Scottish Labour MP was booed when she suggested that it was immoral to deploy Trident. When nuclear weapons were discussed in the Edinburgh parliament, in 2006 and 2007, almost the only argument made in favour of Trident was that it created jobs. The tone of the response in the Scottish debates ranged from grudging acceptance to angry resistance.

On 25 January Scottish Green Party MSP Patrick Harvie asked the First Minister if he would promise not to do a deal that would mean Trident remaining in Scotland. Alex Salmond replied: "It is inconceivable that an independent nation of 5.25 million people would tolerate the continued presence of weapons of mass destruction on its soil."[35]

Philip Hammond's suggestion, that he would force an independent Scotland to pay for an expensive new nuclear base in some, as yet unidentified, corner of England's green and pleasant land, shows a serious failure to understand the place of nuclear weapons in Scotland's recent political history.

Notes

1. BBC Radio 4 lunchtime news 19 January 2012

2. BBC Radio 4 lunchtime news 19 January 2012

3. Coulport and Successor Systems Richard Mottram PS/PUS 13 July 1979 The National Archives (TNA) DEFE 24-2122 e53. Thanks are due to Brian Burnell for his research into National Archive records on the history of the British nuclear weapons programme.

4. "Would this effectively lead us into unilateral disarmament because the costs of replicating the ship lift, the explosive handling jetty, the big storage facility at Coulport, would be billions and we would have to think of where that was put?" Admiral West speaking on Radio 4, quoted in the Daily Record, 30 December 2011.

5. Uncharted Waters: The UK, nuclear weapons and the Scottish question, Malcolm Chalmers and William Walker, Tuckwell Press, 2001

6. Naval Ballistic Missile Force: Report of Working Party established by SMBA 5268, 25 February 1963, TNA ADM 1-28965 (Working Party Report); Uncharted Waters Chalmers and Walker.

7. http://hansard.millbanksystems.com/written_answers/1981/jul/14/trident-coulport-base

8. Successor system to Polaris JF Howe DFA(P) 5 June 1979 TNA DEFE 24-2122 e28

9. Nuclear Matters: Questions for the USA, Richard Mottram PS/PUS 6 July 1979 TNA DEFE 24-2122 e46

10. Coulport and Successor Systems Michael Quinlan DUS(P) 11 July 1979 TNA DEFE 24-2122 e52

11. http://hansard.millbanksystems.com/written_answers/1981/jul/14/trident-coulport-base

12. A detailed proposal to transfer Trident C4 missile maintenance work to the US had already been drafted. The only issue had been whether this would be an interim or

permanent arrangement.

13. A radiological probabilistic risk assessment of the Faslane shiplift for Vanguard class submarines with Strategic Weapon System embarked, AWE Aldermaston, November 2000. Obtained by Scottish CND under the Freedom of Information Act.

14. US Government Bill of Lading GBL G-4432893, 1 September 1988, quoted in Trident D5 Missile Explosive Propellant Hazards, Glen Milner, Ground Zero Campaign, July 2001.

15. http://www.mod.uk/NR/rdonlyres/B1415470-BC8B-47E1-90C0-E206AF6748A0/0/tt133_dec07.pdf

16. Uncharted Waters Chalmers and Walker

17. Successor system to Polaris JF Howe DFA(P) 5 June 1979 TNA DEFE 24-2122 e28

18. Coulport and Successor Systems Michael Quinlan DUS(P) 11 July 1979 TNA DEFE 24-2122 e52

19. Coulport and Successor Systems Richard Mottram PS/PUS 13 July 1979 TNA DEFE 24-2122 e53

20. "We should not delude ourselves that showing the difficulties in all other alternatives will lead to the conclusion that a 'greenfield' site is acceptable". TNA DEFE 24-2122 e53

21. Working Party Report; Uncharted Waters Chalmers and Walker.

22. http://www.nationaltrust.org.uk/antony/

23. Working Party Report; Uncharted Waters Chalmers and Walker.

24. http://www.visitmyharbour.com/viewchart.asp?chart=16D26C3458CF22320

25. Working Party Report; Uncharted Waters Chalmers and Walker.

26. http://www.publications.parliament.uk/pa/cm200607/cmselect/cmdfence/ucwhite/ucm402.htm

27. Philip Hammond speaking on Radio 4, 18 January 2012

28. Admiral West speaking on Radio 4, quoted in the Daily Record, 30 December 2011

29. Robertson slams SNP for 'reckless' defence plan. Herald, 21 January 2012

30. http://wws.princeton.edu/research/cases/ukraine.pdf

31. http://wikimapia.org/6408751/Underground-Submarine-base-Nuclear-warheads-storage-Now-museum.

32. http://www.telegraph.co.uk/news/uknews/defence/9043092/Nuclear-subs-will-stay-in-Scotland-Royal-Navy-chiefs-decide.html

33. Processing of UK Trident missiles in the US, British Embassy Wasthington, MJE Fretwell, 3 December 1981, TNA DEFE 24-2123 e21

34. ibid

35. Official Record, Scottish Parliament 25 January 2012.

Disarming Trident

A practical guide to de-activating and dismantling the Scottish-based Trident nuclear weapons system

John Ainslie

Disarming Trident *was published in June 2012 by Scottish CND and Scotland's for Peace.*

Fifty years after the Cuban Missile Crisis, Britain still has large numbers of nuclear weapons poised to destroy Moscow, or any other target chosen by the Ministry of Defence. Moving away from this towards disarmament is not an impossible dream. There are practical steps that can be taken within a short timescale. We don't need to wait for many years.

In the event of Scottish independence, the Parliament in Edinburgh would have the legal right to require the London government to remove nuclear weapons from Scotland. Holyrood could establish a timetable for the de-activation of Trident, within days and weeks, followed by the removal of all nuclear warheads from Scotland within two years. The Scottish government could verify that these measures had been taken.

In the event of a decision by an independent Scottish Government to call for the removal of nuclear weapons there would be no reason for them to delay. There is nowhere for Trident to be moved to. Any postponement would encourage the Remainder of the United Kingdom (RUK) to put pressure on the Scottish Government in the hope that their policy would change.

In a UK context, if the Labour or Conservative parties changed their policy and became serious about abolishing nuclear weapons, then a UK government could use the proposals in this paper as a blueprint for disarmament. They could first ensure that British nuclear weapons could not be used in anger and then they could dismantle all nuclear warheads within four years.

June 2012

* * *

	Action	Timescale
Phase 1	End operational deployment of submarines	7 days
Phase 2	Remove keys and triggers	7 days
Phase 3	Disable missiles	8 days
Phase 4	Remove warheads from submarines	8 weeks
Phase 5	Remove missiles from two submarines	10 weeks
Phase 6	Disable nuclear warheads and remove Limited Life Components from Scotland	1 year
Phase 7	Remove nuclear warheads from Scotland	2 years
Phase 8	Dismantle nuclear warheads	4 years

▲ Disarming Trident - Timetable

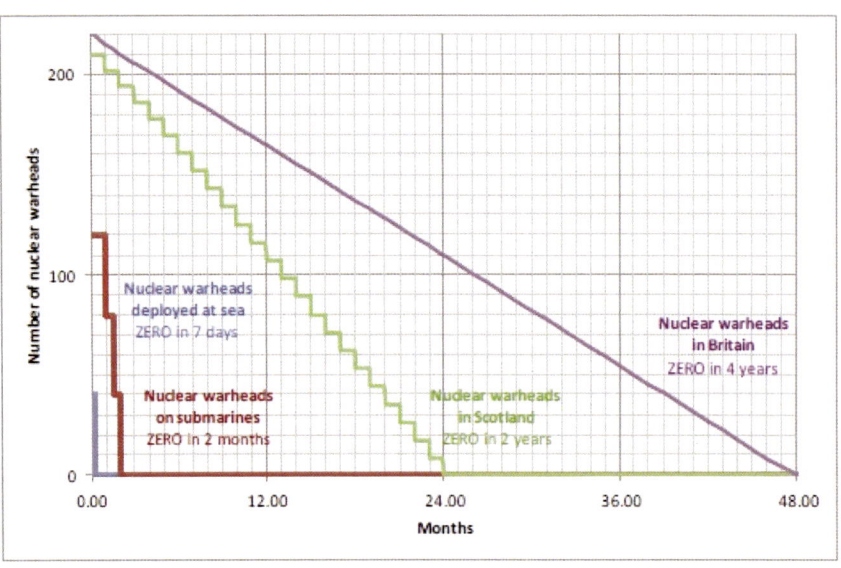

▲ Disarming Trident - Nuclear warhead numbers

Phase One – End operational deployment of submarines

The Royal Navy has four Vanguard class nuclear submarines. There is always one submarine undergoing refit at Devonport. The remaining three vessels are normally armed with Trident missiles and nuclear warheads.[1] One submarine is deployed on patrol. This study assumes a starting point where one vessel is on patrol, the second is on trials and the third is berthed at Faslane.

UK Trident submarines carry out operational patrols, fully armed, which last around 10 weeks. The vessel on patrol is formally on "several days" notice to fire. At any time the alert state could be covertly raised to 15 minutes notice to fire (SQ2) and remain at this higher state for the duration of the patrol.

The first step that could be taken would be to end the current practice of continuous patrols and to stop all operational deployment of Trident submarines. Nuclear submarines can travel long distances at speeds greater than 20 knots. The submarine on patrol could return to Faslane within about 7 days.

Phase Two – Remove keys and triggers

To launch a Trident missile, the Captain turns a key and the Weapons Engineering Officer (WEO) presses a trigger. The key and trigger are kept in separate safes on the submarine. As an initial disarmament step, these keys and triggers could be identified, removed from all submarines and stored in a secure site on shore. This could be carried out immediately for the submarine berthed at Faslane, and shortly after each of the other two vessels returned to port.[2]

Inspectors could place seals on the appropriate parts of the Fire Control System and the storage site. Continuous monitoring could be established at the storage site.

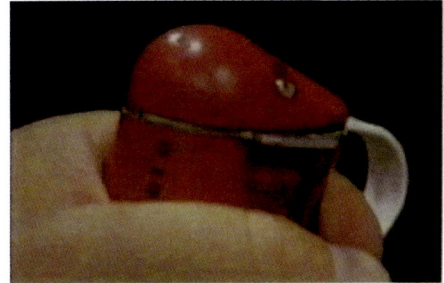
▲ Trigger on HMS Victorious (BBC)

Phase Three – Disable missiles

There is a hatch in each missile tube which enables technicians to replace certain components on the missile while it is on the submarine. These parts include the guidance system and flight control system. Spare guidance and flight control components are stored in the Strategic Weapon System (SWS) building at Faslane. If these parts are removed then the missile can no longer be deliberately launched at any target.

▲ Removable Mark 6 Guidance Unit for a Trident D5 missile (Charles Stark Draper Laboratory)

These components are replaced on a routine basis. Following the Strategic Defence and Security Review of 2010, each Vanguard class submarine carries eight Trident missiles. The removal of vital components from one missile takes around 90 minutes.[3] Eight missiles could probably be disabled within one day.

Similar components could be removed from any spare missiles stored in the Ready Issue Magazines at Coulport. Inspectors could set up seals on the missile access hatches. The components could either be stored in the existing room within the SWS building at Faslane or at another suitable site. Seals and continuous monitoring could be set up at the store.

Phase Four – Remove nuclear warheads from submarines
RNAD Coulport has the facilities and equipment required to load and unload nuclear warheads from Trident missiles. It retains a team of specially trained and experienced personnel to carry out this work. To remove the warheads, each submarine would be taken, in turn, to the Explosives Handling Jetty (EHJ). Once securely berthed in the jetty, the warheads would be removed from the missiles while they were on the submarine.

Current practice is that the unloading of all the warheads on a submarine takes place once every three years, in the pre-refit period. Complete loading also takes place once every three years, at the end of the post-refit work up. In addition, small numbers of warheads are removed from one or two missiles several times each year, when operational submarines dock in the EHJ.

The removal of all 40 warheads from one submarine would take between 7 and 10 days.[4] In theory 120 warheads could be removed from the three armed submarines within one month. In practice this may take longer. There are detailed safety and security procedures for de-mating warheads from missiles and for moving warheads between the EHJ and the Reentry Body Magazines (RBMs) at Coulport. Additional preparation and training may be required prior to conducting unloading on the scale required. This could increase the total time required to eight weeks. Inspectors could monitor the unloading process and establish seals and monitors in the RBMs.

▲ Explosives Handling Jetty Coulport (Scottish CND)

Phase Five – Remove missiles from submarines

▲ Explosives Handling Jetty Coulport (Scottish CND)

Missiles can be removed from submarines in the EHJ. The Ready Issue Magazines (RIMs) at Coulport can only store 16 missiles. Each submarine currently carried eight missiles. It should be possible to store the missiles from two submarines, separately from the nuclear warheads, on-shore at Coulport. This would leave a further eight missiles on the third submarine.

Removing the missiles from one submarine could take up to one week and would only take place after the warheads had been removed. Inspectors could seal and monitor the 16 missiles which had been moved into the RIMs. Monitoring the remaining unarmed missiles on the submarine would be more difficult.

▲ Re-entry Body Process Building, Coulport (Google)

Phase Six – Disable nuclear warheads and remove Limited Life Components from Scotland

A Trident warhead contains three Limited Life Components – the Arming Fuzing and Firing System (AF&F), Gas Transfer System and Neutron Generator.[5] These items are routinely replaced in the Re-entry Body Process Building at Coulport.

Removal of these components would disable the warheads. The weapon cannot be triggered without the AF&F and Neutron Generator. Removing the Gas Transfer System would substantially reduce the warhead's yield. The removal of Limited Life Components from Trident warheads would render them ineffective.

In addition to the 120 "operationally-available" warheads, which are normally deployed on submarines, there are around 100 additional warheads at Coulport. In line with US practice, it is likely that some of these spare warheads will not have their Limited Life Components fitted.

Removing these components from the entire warhead stockpile at Coulport might take around one year. The components are less dangerous than the warheads themselves and so they are easier to transport. Although removing these components may be time consuming, transporting them out of Scotland could be carried out quickly. Inspectors could monitor and verify the removal and storage of Limited Life Components and their transport out of Scotland.

  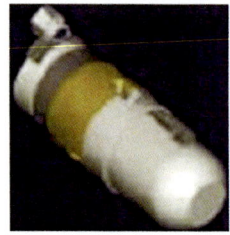

▲ Limited Life Components of a UK Trident warhead
Left: Arming, Fuzinf and Firing System, Centre: Gas Transfer System, Right: Neutron Generator (www.sandia.gov)

Phase Seven – Remove nuclear warheads from Scotland

The physical removal of nuclear warheads from Coulport would be a clear and significant step. When Chevaline was withdrawn from service in the 1990s, some of the warheads were initially stored at RAF Honington in Suffolk, prior to being dismantled at Burghfield. The removal of Trident nuclear warheads from Scotland could be accelerated if some of the warheads were moved to Honington for temporary storage.

The Special Ammunition Site (SAS) at RAF Honington has six Igloo bunkers and 19 older bunkers. Each Igloo can store a significant number of nuclear weapons. During the 1970s large numbers of RAF and Royal Navy nuclear weapons were stored at Honington.[6]

▲ Special Ammunition Site RAF Honington (Google)

Today RAF Honington plays a significant nuclear role as the home of the MOD's main Chemical Biological, Radiological and Nuclear warfare unit. It is no longer a base for fixed-wing aircraft but is a major centre for the RAF Regiment. Assuming the nuclear store at Honington is not currently operational, a number of steps would be required to re-activate it. These would include reviews of safety and security, improved security measures and the deployment of a small team of warhead experts from Coulport and Aldermaston/Burghfield.

Nuclear weapons are routinely moved between Coulport and AWE Burghfield in convoys. It would require 24 convoys, with 8-9 warheads each, to transport the entire stockpile out of Scotland to Honington and/or Burghfield. In the 1980s and 1990s there were periods when convoys were travelling regularly to Scotland once every four to six weeks. During this time additional convoys were transporting nuclear weapons around England. If convoys were travelling at four week intervals then it would take two years to remove the entire stockpile. Inspectors could monitor and verify the removal of nuclear warheads from Scotland.

▲ Nuclear weapons convoy (www.nukewatch.org.uk)

Phase Eight – Dismantle nuclear warheads

The only site in the UK that can disassemble nuclear warheads, including their Nuclear Explosives Package, is the Atomic Weapons Establishment (AWE) Burghfield in Berkshire. There are four assembly/disassembly cells in the existing facility. AWE are building a replacement building, Project Mensa, which will enter service in 2016. It will have a similar capability and probably four assembly/disassembly cells.[7]

Dismantling a Trident warhead at Burghfield would involve the following steps:
1. Prepare cells for disassembly
2. Inspect warhead
3. Remove RV shroud
4. Cut and disconnect detonator cables
5. Remove firing set and neutron generator (if not removed at Coulport)

6. Cut open and remove radiation case
7. Remove primary
8. Remove secondary
9. Prepare for removal of High Explosive (primary)
10. Remove High Explosive (primary)
11. Package plutonium pit (primary)
12. Dismantle secondary [8]

The past workload at Burghfield provides a guide to how long it might take to dismantle the current stockpile of warheads. The planned rate for the production for WE-177 and Chevaline nuclear warheads was 36 per year.[9] In 1981 it was assumed that Trident warheads would be manufactured at a rate of up to 60 per year. Actually assembly probably peaked at around 40 Trident warheads per year. WE-177 and Chevaline warheads were all dismantled by 1998 and 2002 respectively. Disassembly rates for these two weapons were probably between 20 and 40 per year.

These rates were achieved while Burghfield was assembling, refurbishing and disassembling more than one type of warhead at the same time. If all four cells at Burghfield were set up for Trident disassembly then higher rates, perhaps 50-60 warheads per year, could be achieved. On this basis, it would take around 4 years to dismantle the current stockpile of less than 225 warheads.

▲ AWE Burghfield. The four assembly/disassembly cells are visible from their circular contour (Google)

The output from disassembly at Burghfield would be the separated components of a nuclear warhead, including the plutonium pit. Further work would be required to convert the pit into a form where it could not be reconstituted into a nuclear weapon.

Additional Steps

Two further measures could be taken:

Return of Trident missiles to the US: The D5 missiles were initially loaded onto British submarines at the US Navy Trident facility at Kings

Bay, Georgia. They would have to be returned to this site, or possibly the US Navy's other Trident base at Bangor in the Pacific. D5 missiles are currently only transported by sea on Vanguard class submarines. As an alternative, it might be possible to dismantle Trident missiles at Coulport and then to destroy the components. However, this would require the construction of new facilities on the site.

Dismantling Vanguard class submarines: Some Trident-related equipment on submarines could be dismantled while the vessels were at Faslane. For example, much of the Fire Control System and replaceable elements of the launch system could be removed.

The fuel core in the reactor of a Vanguard class submarine reactor can only be removed at 9 Dock in Devonport dockyard. The fourth Trident submarine HMS *Vengeance* is in 9 Dock for a three year refit and refuelling which began in 2012. After this, the MOD plan to carry out refits, without refuelling, on some of the other Trident submarines. This refit programme could be replaced with the defueling and decommissioning of these vessels.

Questions of where and how the final dismantlement of nuclear submarines should be carried out are the subject of the Ministry of Defence's Submarine Dismantling Project.

▲ HMS Vigilant in 9 Dock at Devonport (www.defpro.com)

Verification

Norway, Russia, the US, the UK, the IAEA and NGOs have all been involved in research into how to verify that nuclear disarmament has taken place.[10] Most of this work has focused on dismantling nuclear warheads (phase 8). The principles which have been established can also be applied to the earlier steps.

Britain and Norway collaborated in three exercises, between 2007 and 2011, which explored how a Non Nuclear Weapon State (NNWS) could verify that another country had dismantled its nuclear weapons. This UK-Norway Initiative was founded on the principle that NNWS can play an important role in verifying disarmament. In the event of Scottish independence, Scotland could play a similar role, confirming that the Trident system had been de-activated and that nuclear warheads had been removed from Scotland.

There is an underlying conflict between the NNWS's requirement for evidence and the Nuclear Weapons State's desire to keep information secret, partly to prevent the proliferation of nuclear weapons technology. In the case of the UK Trident system, this is complicated by the fact that many of the classified components are of US origin.

The UK-Norway Initiative established that it is possible for two parties to agree on an Information Barrier which would indicate whether or not a package contained a nuclear weapon without disclosing classified details of the weapon.

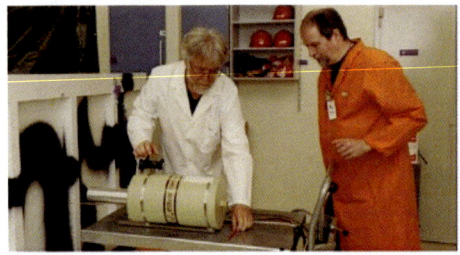

▲ Information Barrier at the Norwegian Disarmament Test Site[11]

With regard to ending the deployment at sea of Trident submarines (phase 1), it is easy to monitor the movement of Trident submarines in and out of Faslane and Coulport. This would provide a basis for establishing that continuous patrols had ended. It would be harder to prove that vessels were not carrying out occasional *ad hoc* patrols.

Verification of the initial de-activation steps, removal of keys/triggers and missile components (phases 2 and 3), might be limited. It would be feasible to establish a process of identifying these items, numbering them and placing them in monitored storage. However, these components are classified. An inspector would be unable to verify that each item was what it appeared to be. Radioactive monitoring would not be effective, because the parts don't contain nuclear material. Further research could be done, in advance, to develop a process which might improve the inspectors' confidence, without disclosing classified information.

Trident missiles can carry a mix of warheads and inert Re-entry Vehicles.[12] The latter are added to swamp the Moscow ABM system. The inert RVs look very similar to a warhead. With regard to the US Trident system, the START agreement allowed Russia to occasionally inspect a sample of submarines and to check whether there were missiles in specific launch tubes. The agreement did not, however, provide a way that Russian inspectors could check how many warheads were on each missile.

This suggests that it would be difficult for an external inspector to count the warheads on a UK Trident missile. However, an inspector could verify that all warheads and inert RVs had been removed (phase 4). To do this, the nose-cone of the missile would be removed and shrouds placed over the third stage and the Release Assembly fittings. In this way, it would be possible to show that there were no warheads or inert RVs present, without disclosing classified information about the missile's design.

There is a second way in which the removal of warheads from a submarine could be verified. An Information Barrier, as proposed in the UK-Norway Initiative, could be used to confirm when warheads were moved out of the Explosives Handling Jetty, after unloading. This technology would enable the NNWS (Scotland) to discriminate between nuclear warheads and inert RVs without inspecting them visually.

Monitoring warheads from when they were taken off each submarine would give greater confidence that later disarmament measures were comprehensive. This would establish the Chain of Custody at an early point in the process.

In order to verify the removal of missiles from submarines into the Ready Issue Magazines (phase 5), the inspectors would require a level of access similar to that which the United States gave to Russian officials under the START agreement.

Monitoring the removal of the Tritium Reservoir, one of the Limited Life Components (phase 6) should be possible, because it contains radioactive material. An external inspector might be able to distinguish between a box containing a real tritium reservoir and a similar box which does not, without seeing the reservoir itself. This process could also be used to monitor the transport of Tritium Reservoirs out of Scotland. The Neutron Generator contains a small amount of tritium and so the same approach might be possible. Identifying Arming, Fuzing and Firing systems, without classified access, would be more difficult.

The removal of nuclear warheads from Scotland (phase 7) could be verified using an Information Barrier. This would allow an NNWS (Scottish) inspector to verify whether or not a container held a warhead, before it was placed in a lorry.

The verification of warhead disassembly (phase 8) has been the focus of significant research. A 1997 US study concluded that "moderate inspector confidence in the dismantlement of a nuclear

▲ Workers inspect a US W76 warhead (www.sandia.gov)

warhead is achievable without the need for two sides to engage in an exchange of classified information".[13]

In May 2002 the UK carried out an exercise which demonstrated that external inspectors could be given Managed Access to the warhead assembly/disassembly site at Burghfield. In a subsequent paper the UK concluded that "managed inspector access to sensitive nuclear warhead facilities, done properly, is able to permit some degree of access for non-security cleared personnel."[14]

The first exercises in the UK-Norway Initiative assumed that there was a good relationship and collaboration between the two parties. The third exercise was based on a scenario where there was greater hostility and suspicion. The NNWS had less confidence that disarmament had taken place where the underlying relationship was tense than when it was more friendly.

Some elements of an effective verification regime could be set up more quickly than others. Monitoring the presence of submarines at Faslane would be straightforward. Inspecting a missile, to confirm that all warheads and inert RVs had been removed, need not be a complex undertaking. This, and similar steps, would be easier if the United States government adopted a positive approach to the process. Developing Information Barriers could take some time. Delays to the timetable could be avoided if processes were established and experts identified before Day One. Alternatively, the more robust verification measures might only be introduced in the later stages of disarmament.

Security, Heath and Safety

There are Health and Safety risks associated with these disarmament steps. However, the overall effect of this plan would be to reduce risks to the workforce and the general public. When Trident is dismantled, whether sooner or later, there will be risks associated with the movement and disassembly of nuclear warheads. If this is done earlier, then we will avoid the additional risks from keeping the system in service. If Trident is kept on patrol and nuclear warheads are upgraded then the risks will be greater. De-activating and dismantling Trident as soon as possible eliminates these avoidable risks.

The plan to remove all nuclear warheads from submarines within eight weeks and to transport them in a series of convoys over a two year period would raise security issues. However, the risk of a terrorist attack would be lower than normal because this was clearly part of a disarmament initiative.

Disarming Trident after Scottish independence

A prohibition of nuclear weapons, or all Weapons of Mass Destruction, could be written into the constitution of an independent Scotland. In its constitution, the Philippines "adopts and pursues a policy of freedom from nuclear weapons in its territory".[15] Austria has a passed a constitutional Act which says that "nuclear weapons must not be manufactured, stored, transported, tested or used in Austria".[16] Mongolia has an act which prohibits any individual or state from stationing or transporting nuclear weapons on its territory.[17] Legislation in New Zealand goes further and prohibits any person from aiding or abetting the manufacture, possession or control over nuclear weapons.[18]

The Government of an independent Scotland could set out a short, but realistic, timetable for disarmament. This would cover the de-activation of nuclear weapons and their removal from Scotland (phases 1-7). They could also recommend that the warheads were then completely dismantled (phase 8) in England.

This stance would enable Scotland to play a proper role as a responsible state implementing international law, in the light of the International Court of Justice opinion (1996) that "the threat or use of nuclear weapons would generally be contrary to the rules of international law applicable in armed conflict". It would also be consistent with calls from the General Assembly of the United Nations and the Non-Proliferation of Nuclear Weapons Treaty review conference (2010) for progress towards nuclear disarmament.

Practical implementation of these disarmament measures would largely be the responsibility of the Remainder of the United Kingdom (RUK). However, the Scottish Government should be able to verify that action had been taken.

The Government of an independent Scotland would be keen to establish positive relations with countries around the world and with RUK. Calling for the rapid de-activation and removal of nuclear weapons is not inconsistent with this. It would be a clear signal that Scotland intended to position itself as a forward-looking progressive member of international society, actively seeking to help the international community to achieve one of its objectives, the elimination of Weapons of Mass Destruction.

Notes

This paper complements *Trident: Nowhere to Go*, a Scottish CND/CND report published in January 2012 which demonstrated that there were no viable alternative locations for Trident to be moved to, either in the UK or abroad.

1. There is a gap of up to 12 months between when a submarine leaves refit and when it becomes operational. During this time there are only 2 operational submarines.
2. It would be possible to accelerate this process if keys and triggers were offloaded by helicopter before the submarines berthed.
3. Beyond the Nuclear Shadow, RAND, 2003, http://www.dtic.mil/cgi-bin/GetTRDoc?AD=ADA416560; Bruce G. Blair, Global Zero Alertfor Nuclear Forces (Washington, DC: Brookings Institution), 1995, pp. 88-89.
4. Based on the time taken to initially load warheads on HMS Vanguard in December 1994, prior to its first patrol.
5. In the case of the UK Trident warhead, the AF&F, Gas Transfer System and Neutron Generator are purchased from the United States.
6. In 1972 it was anticipated that the numbers of nuclear bombs at Honington would peak in mid 1976. The actual number has been redacted. The National Archive AIR 2-78147 y, 16 May 1972 . Similar Igloos at US Air Force bases have each stored as many as 50 nuclear bombs. http://www.fas.org/blog/ssp/2009/11/locations.php. In the 1970s the RAF were planning to store around 36 WE177C bombs in two igloos at RAF Laarbruch in Germany. Satellite images show no visible changes to the Honington SAS since warheads were stored there. www.terraserver.com (September 2011 image)
7. A planning application document for Project Mensa referred to Cell A and Cells C. The design is symmetrical and there are probably four identical cells.
8. This is a simplified version of the procedures detailed in the US Department of Energy 1997 study, http:// www.fas.org/sgp/othergov/doe/dis/
9. WE177C production was planned at a rate of 3 per month. The National Archive AIR 2-78147 y, 16 May 1972.
10. US Department of Energy dismantling study, http://www.fas.org/sgp/othergov/doe/dis/UK-Norway Initiative, http://www.mod.uk/DefenceInternet/AboutDefence/CorporatePublications/SecurityandIntelligencePublications/InternationalSecurity/UkNorwayInitiativeOnNuclearWarheadDismantlementVerification.htm
Verifying Warhead Dismantlement: Past, present, future, David Cliff, Hassan Elbahtimy & Andreas Persbo, http:// www.vertic.org/media/assets/Publications/VM9.pdf
11. http://www.norway-un.org/NorwayandUN/Selected_Topics/Disarmament/UK-Norway-Iniatitive-Research-into- the-Verification-of-nuclear-warhead-dismantlement/
12. Current loading is possibly 5 warheads and 7 inert RVs on each UK Trident missile
13. Verifying Warhead Dismantlement, page 13
14. Verifying Warhead Dismantlement, page 61
15. http://www.concourt.am/armenian/legal_resources/world_constitutions/constit/philipin/philip-e.htm
16. http://www.ris.bka.gv.at/Dokumente/Erv/ERV_1999_1_149/ERV_1999_1_149.pdf
17. https://www.unodc.org/tldb/pdf/Mongolia/MON_Nuclear.pdf
18. http://canterbury.cyberplace.org.nz/peace/nukefree.html

The Cuban Missile Crisis and its implications for Scotland

John Ainslie

First published in October 2012, on the 50th anniversary of the crisis, as a Scottish CND Education Pack.

The most dangerous moment in human history[1]

On the evening of Friday 26 October 1962 General Issa Pliyev, Commander of Soviet Forces in Cuba, sent a report to his superiors in Moscow. He was in charge of the large military force, including 160 nuclear weapons, which Nikita Khrushchev had deployed to the island, to "throw a hedgehog down the pants of Uncle Sam".[2] Pliyev was expecting American aircraft to launch a massive bombing campaign at dawn the next day. He ordered the radar systems at Surface to Air Missile (SAM) sites around the island to be switched on for the first time. Nuclear warheads were moved from two central stores and deployed with their missile regiments. Three FKR cruise-missile launchers were moved to their firing position, ready to launch a nuclear attack on the US base at Guantanamo Bay.[3]

The arsenal under Pliyev's control included 36 R-12 missiles which could reach Washington and New York. The R-12 sites had been spotted by US reconnaissance planes on 15 October.[4] The aerial photographs had been displayed at the United Nations and flashed around the world. Then, on 26 October, US intelligence identified several Luna battlefield missiles. The CIA were unable to detect any signs that the Luna missiles were nuclear-armed, but they were. There was a total of 12 of these mobile missiles on the island. In addition, 80 warheads, half of Pliyev's nuclear arsenal, were for FKR cruise missiles. Despite frequent overflights, the American spy planes had spotted only one of the FKR sites and they

▲ Nuclear-armed FKR Cruise Missile in Cuba in October 1962. These missiles were not detected by US intelligence. Photogrpah provided by the Cuban government in 2002.

thought this was a conventional facility. The intelligence analysts also failed to correctly identify the two central stores where most of the nuclear weapons were held. In summary, US military planners grossly underestimated the number of nuclear weapons on the island, particularly the tactical nuclear weapons.

The one American aircraft which flew over Cuba on the morning of Saturday 27th October was not a bomber, but a U-2 reconnaissance plane. Moscow had replied to Pliyev's report by saying that his soldiers could open fire on US aircraft, but only in self-defence. The Russian officers in the Cuban command post thought that the U-2 was identifying targets which would be bombed a few hours later. So they ordered that the plane be attacked by two missiles before it left Cuban airspace.

The downing of this aircraft and the death of the pilot, Rudolf Anderson, brought the crisis to a new level. The American Defense Secretary, Robert McNamara, had for days held at bay his generals, who had from the start been advocating a massive airstrike. Now even McNamara was proposing a counter-attack, at least against the SAM site which had downed Anderson's U-2. Others called for tougher action. US forces were ready to strike Air Defence targets within 2 hours, to launch an all-out bombing campaign within 12 hours and to invade the island within 7 days.

It was not only the invasion force in Florida that was on high alert. US nuclear forces had been moved onto Defence Condition (DEFCON) 3 when President Kennedy addressed the nation on Tuesday 22nd October. The following day Strategic Air Command took its forces up to DEFCON 2. This meant that for 24 hours each day there were 65 B-52 nuclear bombers in the air, circling over the far North of America and the Mediterranean, waiting for their instructions to proceed to targets in the Soviet Union. Over 1,000 other US nuclear bombers were ready for take-off at airfields across the globe. Nuclear missiles were in an advanced state of readiness. In England the RAF had 72 V-bombers loaded with nuclear weapons and ready for take-off in 15 minutes or less. 59 Thor nuclear missiles, under dual Anglo-American control, were prepared for action in East Anglia. Similar forces in the Soviet Union were at a very high state of alert.

The US Air Force was under the command of General Curtis LeMay, architect of the fire-bombing of Tokyo in 1945. LeMay was an outspoken critic of President Kennedy and of McNamara. He chastised them for being too cautious during the crisis. LeMay's attitude to Cuba was "let them fry". LeMay was the model for the character General Jack D Ripper in Stanley Kubrick's film *Dr Strangelove*. General Ripper is a rogue commander who starts a nuclear war.

General Thomas Power, head of Strategic Air Command, was even more militant than LeMay. Power's attitude was that if a nuclear war resulted in two Americans surviving and only one Russian, then the United States had won. Power had covertly been bringing his nuclear forces to a very high state of alert since 20th October.[5]

The crisis on Saturday 27 October deepened further because of an event far from the Caribbean. While Russia and American were confronting each other over Cuba, they both continued with their programmes of nuclear tests. The Russians detonated a nuclear bomb over Novaya Zemlya on 26 October. Hours later an American U-2 plane was sent to the North Pole to monitor for radiation. The pilot, Captain Charles Maultsby, was navigating by the stars. He lost his bearings because of the confusing coloured lights of the Aurora Borealis. Before long, Maultsby strayed deep inside the Soviet Union. He finally realised his error as he heard Russian folk music over his radio.

In Russian minds this flight could easily have been making a final check of targets for the bombers circling over Alaska. Six MIG-16 fighters were scrambled to intercept Maultsby, but they couldn't fly high enough to shoot him down. As he finally turned back towards Alaska, two US F-106 fighters were sent to escort him. Like many others, these F106s had been

▲ Left: B-59 - photograph taken by the US Navy on 28 October 1962.
Right: Captain Vasili Arkhipov

armed with nuclear air-to-air missiles when the alert state was raised to DEFCON 3. They had no conventional weapons. Fortunately the two sets of fighters never came face to face.

On the same day, in the Sargasso Sea a fleet of American warships surrounded the Russian submarine B-59. The US Navy had devised a procedure whereby they would signal that a submarine should surface by dropping several stun grenades in the water. They had informed Moscow of this procedure, but the Soviet Navy refused to acknowledge the message and did not pass it on to their vessels at sea. The crew of B-59 were stressed, exhausted and living in stifling conditions. There were only a few hours of life in the vessel's batteries. The submariners heard the repeated thumping of practice depth charges detonating close to their hull. The US Navy officers who were launching these small bombs had no idea that the diesel-powered submarine was carrying one nuclear torpedo. Captain Valentin Savitsky was confused. Perhaps the third world war has already started, he declared. He agreed with his political officer that the nuclear torpedo should be prepared for action. He felt that if his submarine was to be sunk, at least he would take an American warship down with him. Fortunately there was another senior officer on the submarine, who held the same rank as the Savistky. Captain Vasili Arkhipov refused to go along with his colleagues and he vetoed the order to prepare the nuclear torpedo. Decades later, when this story first became public, Arkhipov was hailed as the man who stopped World War Three. B-59 surfaced and then headed back to Russia.

As this drama unfolded at sea, McNamara was leaving his office in Washington. He turned to an aide and said that he wasn't sure that he would live to see another Saturday night.

Four decades later, McNamara had the chance to meet with key figures from Russia and Cuba who had been involved in the crisis. He was horrified to learn that the world had come far closer to nuclear Armageddon than he, or anyone else, had realised at the time. On Tuesday 16th October, when the Chiefs of Staff had first proposed an immediate attack, their information on the nuclear weapons in Cuba was very limited. Even by the height of the crisis, on Saturday 27th October, US intelligence had failed to detect the nuclear-armed FKR missiles, some of which were aimed at Guantanamo Bay. There were no electronic safeguards preventing the launch of the Russian nuclear weapons in Cuba, or most American nuclear weapons. While Moscow retained authority over the long-range R-12 missiles, Khrushchev's instructions for the tactical nuclear weapons were inconsistent. First he delegated authority over them to Pliyev, then he said that the weapons should not be used without permission from Moscow. Khrushchev also toyed with the idea of saying that he would hand these tactical nuclear weapons over to Cuban control if the island was invaded.

The shooting down of Anderson's U-2 was very significant. Not only did it mark a serious escalation in the crisis, but it also showed how distant leaders could lose control over a conflict. Sitting in Moscow, Khrushchev was worried about a global nuclear war. To him, shooting down the U-2 was rash and dangerously provocative. For the Soviet officers in Cuba, who were waiting for American bombs to fall, attacking the spy plane was a reasonable operational decision.

Had the US Air Force implemented OPLAN 312, an all-out air attack on Cuba, followed by OPLAN 316, an invasion of the islands, then there is no guarantee that the Russian officers who had practical control over individual nuclear weapons, particularly the tactical weapons, would have shown restraint as their comrades were killed by American bombs.

The crisis ended on Sunday 28 October. Khrushchev mistakenly thought that Kennedy was going to make a broadcast to the nation at 9 am, Washington time, saying that the bombing campaign had started. Shortly before this, the Soviet leadership met outside Moscow and agreed to remove their missiles from Cuba in exchange for the withdrawal of American missiles from Turkey.

Living in the shadow of the Cold War

In one way the world is closer to the nuclear apocalypse today than it was on the 27th October 1962. Then most of the nuclear weapons were bombs which would be dropped by aircraft. Each plane would have taken several hours to reach its target. There were far fewer strategic missiles in 1962 than there are today. The United States had 132 Inter Continental Ballistic Missiles (ICBMs), plus 105 Medium Range Ballistic Missiles (MRBMs) in England, Italy and Turkey. The Soviet Union had 42 ICBMs, plus 36 MRBMs in Cuba. The total number of nuclear warheads from missiles that could hit targets in the USA and Soviet Union was 315. All of these missiles had to be fuelled with liquid fuel before they could be launched.

Today the US and Russia between them have 1,700 nuclear warheads on missiles which are on high alert. These could all hit their targets in less than one hour from now. All of the missiles are solid-fuelled, which means they can be launched immediately.

October 1962 was just one of the many times when the world has been poised on the edge of the nuclear apocalypse. For example, on 26 September 1983 Stanislav Petrov sat in Serpukhov-15, the Russian early warning centre, watching as one, two, then ten dots appeared on his screen. Each represented a missile fired from the United States towards the Soviet Union. The Standing Orders said that in this situation Petrov should immediately inform the General Staff Central Command Post at Chekhov-3. Chekhov-3 was able to launch Russia's entire arsenal of ICBMs by remote control, and it can still do this today. Petrov decided to ignore his orders. He did not to pass on the warning. Instead he waited until after the missiles would have exploded. Only then was he able to confirm that the dots were due to a computer failure. Five weeks later, the world was again on the brink of nuclear war. The Soviet Union misinterpreted a NATO nuclear exercise, Able Archer, as the final preparations for a real attack. These dangers did not end with the collapse of the Soviet Union. In 1995, President Yeltsin was on the verge of authorising a nuclear strike, when a Norwegian weather rocket was mistaken for a Trident missile.

Since 1962, one way that the world's nuclear arsenals have changed is that they now rely very heavily on complex computer software. Cyber attacks, and false warnings of cyber attacks, are a greater danger than ever. During the Cuban Missile Crisis a roaming brown bear triggered an alert at an American Air Defense Command post. A guard opened fire on the intruder. The attack was initially interpreted as an act of sabotage, presaging a Soviet assault. Preparations were made to scramble as many jets as possible, so they weren't caught on the ground. Today, the danger is from virtual bears, malevolent or misplaced bytes which could spiral the world into nuclear war by accident.

Scotland

Scotland played a key role in the Cuban missile crisis. In 1962 all five of the US Navy's new Polaris nuclear submarines were based in the Holy Loch. The force had been deployed to the Clyde one year earlier in the face of vigorous protests from across Scotland.

 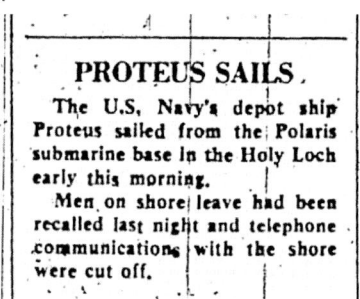

▲ Left: US Polaris submarine, Holy Loch 1962
Right: *Glasgow Herald* 24 October 1962

At the start of October three of the submarines were at sea, on patrol. On 16th October the Joint Chiefs of Staff recommended that the remaining two submarines should be sent to sea. However, this was not initially approved. On 22nd October, President Kennedy placed all nuclear forces on DEFCON 3. The two submarines in Holy Loch were rushed out to sea within 24 hours. Their support ship, USS *Proteus*, also sailed down the Clyde estuary and headed to the North of Scotland. It remained at sea for ten days.

The American fleet has left the Holy Loch, but today there are British submarines, carrying American Trident missiles, based at Faslane. The entire British nuclear arsenal of around 225 nuclear warheads is based in Scotland. There are always 40 nuclear warheads deployed on one Trident submarine at sea, 24/7. If there was a major crisis, then one, and possibly two, other Trident submarines would be quickly sent to sea, as in 1962.

In a landmark speech to the United Nations, President Kennedy said: "Every man, woman and child lives under a nuclear sword of Damocles, hanging by the slenderest of threads, capable of being cut at any moment by accident or miscalculation or by madness. The weapons of war must be abolished before they abolish us."

Five decades later, we have become like villagers living under a volcano, complacent about the risk of sudden catastrophic destruction. But this nuclear danger does not come from the heart of the earth. It is manmade and can be dismantled by human hands.

Notes

1. Arthur Schlesinger, biographer of John F Kennedy described the Cuban Missile Crisis as "the most dangerous moment of human history". The critical day of the crisis was Saturday 27th October.

2. Comment by Khrushchev to his Defence Minister, Rodion Malinovsky, in April 1962. Reported in One Minute to Midnight, Michael Dobbs, which is the main source for this paper, p 47.

3. FKR - Frontovaya Krylataya Raketa - Frontline Cruise Missile. These were radio-controlled missiles for coastal defence. In 1962 US intelligence did not realise that this type of missile had a nuclear capability.

4. The Russian missile men had been ordered to redeploy the R-12s to alternative firing positions, but these were not yet ready.

5. Strategic Air Command Operations in the Cuban Crisis of 1962, Historical Study No 90, Volume 1, Strategic Air Command.

Substandard

The Trident whistleblower and the safety of British submarines

John Ainslie

This report, first published on Scottish CND's website on 28 May 2015, shortly after AB McNeilly's own report appeared, placed McNeilly's revelations 'in the context of known safety issues with British nuclear submarines'. With John's agreement, it was also published in Spokesman 129 (available online).

On 17 May 2015 the *Sunday Herald* published serious allegations of safety and security weaknesses on Britain's Trident submarines.[1] The article was based on an 18-page report from Able Seaman William McNeilly.[2] McNeilly was training to be a missile technician on a Trident submarine and had been onboard HMS *Victorious* throughout its patrol from January to April 2015. He said 'the Trident programme is a disaster waiting to happen'.[3]

This report places McNeilly's allegations in the context of known safety issues with British nuclear submarines. Individual incidents on submarines have briefly attracted media attention – HMS *Astute* running aground on Skye, the collision between a British and French submarine, a nuclear powered submarine stranded in Gibraltar for one year. However, these episodes slip quickly from the public mind. The list of problems here is long, but not comprehensive, because one recurring feature of nuclear submarines is secrecy.

Summary

McNeilly's report brings together descriptions of what he saw onboard HMS *Victorious* and accounts that he heard of incidents and problems on other nuclear submarines. He outlines safety concerns, defects, security breaches and careless practice.

Official reports show that the Navy does not have enough Suitably Qualified and Experienced submariners to operate the Trident missile system or the reactors on nuclear submarines and that the greatest risk to the safety of the Defence Nuclear Programme comes from a shortage of personnel. An overemphasis on operational requirements, at the expense of safety, has contributed to a number of submarine incidents in recent years.

The Trident missile was designed in a way that introduces a greater risk than other types of nuclear missile. Between 2009 and 2012, fires on British nuclear submarines took place at a rate of around one every six weeks. Problems identified in a fire on one submarine in 2004 were repeated in a subsequent fire two-and-a-half years later. There are 13 known collisions involving British nuclear submarines and 11 incidents when submarines have run aground. There have been three major generic defects with the reactor designs on British nuclear submarines. These were discovered in 1989, 2000 and 2012.

There is an unacceptable risk of a terrorist attack on a Trident submarine in the Faslane shiplift and there have been instances of sabotage on submarines in service with other navies. The reactors on British submarines are much less reliable than those on American submarines. This means that there is a significant risk that a submarine could go into an uncontrolled dive.

Summary of allegations made by William McNeilly
Safety concerns

McNeilly repeats a report he heard of a fire in the Missile Compartment of a Trident submarine. Toilet rolls, stacked in the Missile Compartment, caught fire. This filled several of the decks of the compartment with smoke. The crew struggled to bring the incident under control and had difficulty using their breathing apparatus.

▲ Able Seaman William McNeilly

Despite this earlier incident, McNeilly says that the risk of a fire in the Missile Compartment wasn't taken seriously. A major fire in the missile area can only be brought under control by flooding the compartment with nitrogen. However, he said that the nitrogen cylinders were significantly below the required pressure. Restrictions on personal electronic equipment, which could trigger an electrical fire, were not enforced. McNeilly told his superiors about rubbish near the missiles, which could have caused a fire, but no action was taken.

He was concerned about the risk of an electrical fire. He says no attempt was made to isolate electrical equipment after a leak was detected in the

Riders' Mess (Riders are extra personnel on the vessel). There were serious problems with condensation in parts of the submarine. A sprinkler system was accidentally activated in the torpedo room. Some of the personal electronic equipment used by submariners had not been PAT tested.

Crew members who work on the Trident missile system should have a thorough knowledge of CB8890, the manual for Trident safety and security. However, McNeilly's exam on the manual was a sham. Some who missed the test were allocated results at random.

The status of the Trident missiles is monitored at the Control and Monitoring Panel (CAMP), but this was not always manned. An audible alarm on the panel was muted because it was going off repeatedly. A second recurring alarm in the Missile Control Compartment, due to a problem with power from one of the Turbo Generators, was also ignored.

One of the more hazardous operations conducted by missile engineers is the insertion of DC/AC inverters in the missiles before a patrol and their removal after a patrol. To do this they have to open a hatch in each missile tube and gain direct access to the missiles. McNeilly describes how the removal of inverters at the end of their patrol was rushed and they did not follow the written procedures or the practice used on US submarines.

▲ Installing inverters on a Trident missile onboard a US submarine[4]

Other safety issues identified by McNeilly are:

- There was a list of defects on the Trident missile system on HMS *Victorious* and the list was almost full.
- One of the decks in the Missile Compartment was used as a gym and weights were thrown and dropped near missile equipment.
- Extra beds blocked access to DC switch boards and a hydraulics isolation valve.
- Use of banned substance in cleaning material, causing problems with fumes.
- There was an incident when a generator compartment was flooded on a submarine and this could have resulted in the loss of the vessel if it had been handled differently.

Defects on Trident submarines

McNeilly says that at the end of the patrol they tested the Missile Compensation System on HMS *Victorious*. This system should quickly restore the balance of the submarine after a missile is launched, to enable each subsequent missile to be fired. The test was carried out three times and each time the test failed.

The missile hatches on the submarine are powered by the Main Hydraulic Plant. At the end of the patrol they should have tested that they would have been able to open the hatches if required. But they were unable to conduct the test because of seawater in the hydraulic system.

These two problems meant that they could not confirm that the submarine could have launched its missiles when on patrol.

McNeilly says that there was noise from the diving planes when the vessel submerged at the start of its patrol and that this was part of a wider problem with diving planes. Jammed planes can lead to the loss of the submarine in an uncontrolled dive.

There were problems with the turbo generators, which provide the main power source, and with one of the diesel generators, which are the back-up power source. The safety of the submarine would be compromised if both sources of electrical power were lost.

In addition to these problems on HMS *Victorious*, McNeilly refers to defects on other submarines. He says that there are currently only two operational Trident submarines, probably due to refit and maintenance cycles, and that there are major defects on both the operational vessels.

▲ HMS *Victorious* under repair at Faslane on 23 May 2015 (bank holiday weekend)

He visited a Trident submarine in the shiplift and many of the items of equipment were tagged with red markers, either for maintenance or defects. When they were told not to touch anything in the submarine's control room, one of the crew responded 'nothing works, you can touch what you like'. Crew members manning the Missile Control Centre said their equipment was all 'f***ed'.

Security breaches

McNeilly revealed two major breaches of security on HMS *Victorious*. Despite not having DV security clearance, he was given access to Top Secret information showing where the submarine was carrying out its patrol. He also says he could have worked out the key to the Weapons Engineering Officer's safe when he watched him enter the combination. This would have given the junior crew member unauthorised access to the trigger which launches Trident missiles. In addition, McNeilly was told of an officer who frequently left Top Secret documents lying on his bed.

McNeilly says there was a lack of adequate security controlling access to Trident submarines. He suggested that it was easier to get into most nightclubs than Faslane.

He gave the following examples of lapsed security:

- The QM sentry (in sentry box at gang plank) was not an effective security check as he routinely lets people pass unchecked.
- Pass checks and gate checks were not thorough. People are able to pass without showing face, especially when it is raining. It is possible for extra people to get in as part of a group. There are lots of missing Navy ID cards circulating.
- Electronic gate access with PIN not working.
- No checks on bags being taken onto submarine by sailors or civilians. He was able to leave his bags next to the missiles on his first visit to a submarine.

Careless practice

McNeilly described how at times, such as the loading of stores before patrol, the submarine was chaotic. At the end of the patrol both the junior ranks' and the senior ranks' toilets were flooded and he notes that this was an apt summary of the state of affairs on this deadly nuclear-armed vessel.

Staffing problems

In his report William McNeilly said 'the rate at which people are getting pushed through the system because of manpower shortages is scary. SWS [Strategic Weapon System] is so short on manpower it's unbelievable and people are getting pushed through at an alarming rate.'

Official documents show that the MOD does not have an adequate number of people operating the Trident missile system. In each of the last three years the MOD's annual reports have identified the Trident Strategic Weapon System as an area where there is a shortage of personnel, known as a 'pinch point'.[5]

Year	Pinch Point Group	Liability	Shortfall	Difference
2012	Strategic Weapon System Control & Monitoring Panel Rank: Leading Hand	30	-	30%
2013	Strategic Weapon System Rank: Senior Rate	120	20	15%
2014	Strategic Weapon System Control & Monitoring Panel Rank: OR4-OR8 [Leading Hand – Chief Petty Officer]	220	55	25%

These reports also show that there are not enough submariners who are qualified to carry out reactor operations. There has been a 15% shortfall in Category A2 nuclear watchkeepers in each of the last three years. The shortfall in Category B nuclear watchkeepers has been between 10% and 15% over the same period. There is also likely to be a shortage of suitably trained and experienced officers for some key posts, but this is not identified in the MOD's annual reports.

The 2014 report from the Defence Nuclear Safety Regulator (DNSR) says that the greatest risk to the safety of the Defence Nuclear Programme (DNP) is the lack of Suitably Qualified and Experienced Personnel (SQEP) – 'The difficulties in maintaining a sustainable community of suitable nuclear competent staff has been, and is again, raised by DNSR as the principal risk to maintaining safety in the DNP'.[7] The regulator has made similar remarks each year since 2006 and has identified the attractions of alternative employment in the civil sector as a contributing factor. The 2008/09 safety report for the Clyde Naval Base said that human factors were the principal root cause of 70% of nuclear safety events.[8]

Lack of training and experience has been a factor in a number of nuclear submarine incidents. One reason that HMS *Astute* ran aground on Skye in October 2010 was that the Officer Of the Watch did not have suitable experience for carrying out a boat transfer in the dark in an unfamiliar area.[9] The Board of Inquiry report into the grounding also points out that lack of a chart on the bridge combined with ineffective supervision, 'effectively resulted in the control of navigation resting with a Leading Seaman'.[10]

Manning issues contributed to HMS *Triumph* running aground off the West coast of Scotland in November 2000. The Board of Inquiry found 'evidence that the supervision of very inexperienced Control Room Watchkeepers was, at times, inadequate'.[11] 30% of the crew were new to the vessel. Two officers implicated in the incident, the Officer Of the Watch and the Second Officer of the Watch, had only joined the submarine shortly before it sailed.

A lack of relevant training contributed to HMS *Tireless* colliding with an iceberg in 2003. While specific training was mandatory if a submarine was due to be deployed under pack ice, there was no similar requirement for deployment in the Marginal Ice Zone.[12] Fleet Headquarters had not given adequate consideration to the hazards from icebergs in this zone and no under-ice training was arranged for *Tireless* before its deployment. The submarine manual, SMP 27, gave the false impression that the submarine's passive sonar can reliably detect icebergs. The crew on *Tireless* assumed that this was correct, but their sonar system gave no advance warning of the iceberg which they hit.

▲ Missile Control and Monitoring Panel Watch on a US Trident Submarine[6]

The lack of trained personnel was also a factor leading to the very poor standards of radioactive waste management at Faslane which were identified in a 2009 report, following a succession of coolant leaks from submarine reactors. The Scottish Environmental Protection Agency was so concerned about poor practice at the site that a spokesman told *Channel 4 News* that if Faslane had been a civil nuclear facility they would have shut it down.

Balance between operational and safety considerations

McNeilly asserts that HMS *Victorious* was sent on patrol when it was not in a suitable condition. In a series of incidents it has been apparent that safety has been compromised because of an overemphasis on operational requirements. In December 1987, a Polaris missile was subject to 'adverse shock' during a handling accident while it was being loaded onto HMS *Repulse* at Coulport. The Board of Inquiry found that 'excessive pressure was put on staff' to undertake the operation due to 'an urgent need to exchange the missile'.[13]

There have been a number of serious accidents during Perisher courses, training submarine commanders, where the focus was on providing realistic operational training rather than on safety. In 1990 HMS *Trenchant* sank the Fishing Vessel *Antares* with the loss of four lives. Officers on the submarine were concentrating on a warship which was

▲ Fishing Vessel *Antares* which was sunk, with the loss of four lives, by HMS *Trenchant* in 1990

exercising with them and failed to take due account of the fishing boat nearby. *Trenchant* incorrectly reported that, although a net had snagged, the fishing vessel was safe. The submarine continued with its exercise and search and rescue alert was only made eight hours later.[14] In 2002, HMS *Trafalgar* ran aground near Fladda-Chuain. Navigation aids were deliberately concealed from the trainee commanders and no back-up navigation system was in place.

In May 2003, HMS *Tireless* collided with an iceberg. The Board of Inquiry concluded, 'The focus of RN submarine environmental effort is in tactical exploitation and there was insufficient focus (HS and on board) on the hazards to submarine safety presented by icebergs'.[15]

On 28 April 2004, 11 crew members refused to go to sea on HMS *Trafalgar* because they regarded the vessel as unsafe. They included 3 out of 4 safety specialists. One of those involved said there were 250 defects on the vessel.

In the early 1990s, the MOD continued to send nuclear-armed Polaris submarines on patrol despite a generic reactor fault which resulted in all other British nuclear-powered submarines being kept in port. The MOD did not fully understand the underlying problem with the reactors until two years after the issue was first noticed. Alan Clark was a Junior Defence Minister at the time. His published diaries show that safety advice was ignored, perhaps by the Defence Minister Tom King (TK) or, more likely, by Mrs Thatcher. Clark's diary entry for 31 Jan 1990 says:

'... news is about to break concerning the trouser-leg fractures in Warspite's cooling system. This could affect every nuclear-powered submarine. The whatever-it-is Authority have already given their advice that we should 'cease to operate' them until the condition is 'rectified'.

'... TK, quite rightly in my view, is continuing to keep the newer ones on station (although whether this is really his decision or was forced on him by the Lady I simply don't know). I suspect the latter because when, sadistically, I rattled him at a meeting, 'If – if there is an accident, it's not just you who resigns; the Government falls', he didn't blench.'[16]

Faslane Peace Camp monitored submarine movements over the next two years. HMS *Resolution* carried out two very long patrols of around 108 days in 1990 and 1991. After the second of these patrols the submarine spent only 6 days at Faslane and then went back on patrol. There was no opportunity to repair defects identified during the patrol or to test the vessel and crew before deployment.

Overemphasis on operational factors, rather than safety, was also a factor in some of the other incidents reported below.

Missile safety

On most types of missile the nuclear warheads are placed on top of the rocket motors. Trident is different. In order to produce a long-range missile which is short enough to fit on a submarine, the nuclear warheads are placed around the third-stage rocket motor. This significantly increases the risk of a catastrophic accident. This weakness was identified by Sidney Drell in a US Government review of nuclear weapons safety published in 1990.

McNeilly quotes paragraphs from the Trident safety manual which confirm this problem. The document refers to Re-entry Bodies (RBs) which is an alternative name for the nuclear warheads.

'When installed in a Trident II D5 missile, RBs clustered around the Third Stage Rocket Motor are at risk from a rocket motor propellant fire'.

'An accident or enemy action may cause rupture of the RB, burning or possible detonation of the HE [High Explosive] and release of radioactive contamination.'

The manual also says that a fire can lead to the detonation of explosives in the nuclear warheads:

'If the HE [High Explosive] charge is exposed to excessive heat without burning, it may become more sensitive and could cook to (non-nuclear) detonation, releasing radioactive materials and aerosols over a wide area'

The risk assessments for the Faslane shiplift assume that the detonation of one missile will result in the explosion of all the missiles onboard a submarine and the dispersal of plutonium from all of the nuclear warheads. The shiplift assessments do not take account of the possibility that a missile explosion could result in the dispersal of radioactive material from the submarine's reactor. However, the manual quoted by McNeilly suggests that this might occur. It says:

'The chief potential hazard associated with a live missile is the accidental ignition of the first, second or third stage rocket motor propellant. If this were to happen in the missile tube with the muzzle hatch shut and locked, the pressure hull and bulkheads of the MC [Missile Compartment] would burst within a matter of seconds'.

If the bulkhead was breached then there is a significant risk that the blast wave or fragments could damage the reactor and possibly trigger the release of radioactive material from the reactor.

Fires on submarines

McNeilly expresses concern that there was inadequate attention on HMS *Victorious* to the potential for water to cause an electrical fire.

▲ Fire damage to HMCS *Chicoutimi* (formerly HMS *Upholder*)

In October 2004 there was a fatal fire onboard HMCS *Chicoutimi*, formerly known as HMS *Upholder*. This British built diesel-powered submarine had been handed over to the Canadian Navy and was in transit from Faslane.[17] Due to inadequate maintenance two hatches had to be kept open while the vessel sailed on the surface in rough seas. 2,000 litres of sea water, from a freak wave, flooded over the coning tower and into the submarine. A short time later this sparked an electrical fire. Within seconds there was very thick black smoke. One officer collapsed and subsequently died. Nine crew members needed treatment for smoke inhalation.

Two-and-a-half years later, in March 2007, there was an explosion and fire on HMS *Tireless* under the Arctic icepack North of Alaska. Two sailors died. The Navy had failed to learn from the fire on *Chicoutimi* and the Damage Control and Fire Fighting (DC&FF) issues were seen a second time. The Board of Inquiry into the fire on *Tireless* said 'Many of the DC&FF lessons identified in the HMCS *Chicoutimi* incident in 2004 have been repeated in this incident'.[18] In both cases the control of fire fighting was difficult because large parts of the submarine were affected by smoke. An identical nozzle detached from a hose in both fires. There were issues with Emergency Breathing Apparatus in both cases. In addition, sailors on

Tireless had not received adequate training to cope with the situation that they faced, in particular attempting to fight a fire from a ladder.

The fire on *Tireless* was caused by the explosion of a Self Contained Oxygen Generator (SCOG). There was a major failure in the assessment of the danger posed by these devices. The Board of Inquiry report said 'There are many systematic failings that contributed to the TIRL explosion which can be collectively viewed as inadequate risk management of the hazards that SCOGs present'.[19]

At the time of the explosion and fire, *Tireless* was operating under the ice pack, North of Alaska. It took three-quarters of an hour for the nuclear-powered submarine to find a gap in the ice and surface. During this period the crew were unable to access the area of the fire because a door had buckled. The incident would have been far worse had it not been for the actions of a surviving member of the crew in the affected area. Despite serious injuries, he was able to dampen down the flames. The Board of Inquiry report said 'The small fire caused by the explosion could easily have taken hold and a major conflagration ensued, with very serious consequences, if xxxxxx had not had the stamina and presence of mind to use all available means to extinguish them'.[20]

McNeilly said that the quality of the speaker system, used to issue safety instructions, was poor. The Board of Inquiry into the fire on *Tireless* noted that this system was inaudible due to noise from the incident. The Cromwell radios onboard were useless. Instructions were passed by word of mouth along the stricken submarine.

McNeilly questioned the rigour of fire drills, pointing out the submariners should be blindfolded to simulate the effects of a fire. The reports from *Chiticoumi*, *Tireless* and other fires show that visibility can be down to a few inches when smoke fills the compartments of a submarine. The report into the *Tireless* fire also found that emergency lighting was inadequate.

Access to Emergency Breathing Apparatus has been a recurring problem in fires on submarines. In April 1992 there was a fire on board HMS *Turbulent* at Devonport. Maintenance work was being carried out on one of the two electrical switchboards when there was a short circuit and a bang followed by a fire. The switchroom is adjacent to the reactor compartment and separated from it by a bulkhead. The Mechanical Engineering Articifer (MEA) of the Watch was not wearing a face mask when he was required to carry out an essential safety task. Petty Officer Christian Checkley removed his face mask and handed it to the MEA. The essential safety task may have been to shut down the reactor. The reactor was producing power at the time of the fire but was quickly shut down. The consequences of the accident might have been much worse if Petty Officer Checkley had not taken this action – for which he received the Queen's Commendation for Bravery. The incident was officially described as 'potentially lethal' and 23 sailors were admitted to hospital suffering from smoke inhalation.

On 19th August 1993 at Devonport, toxic diesel exhaust fumes spread through part of HMS *Torbay*. All 32 sailors who had been on board were taken to hospital. 13 were kept in over the weekend and some were still suffering from the effects of the accident several weeks later. Commenting on the incident, Captain Richard Sharpe, editor of *Jane's Fighting Ships*, said: 'We are dealing with an incredibly small hull which is machinery intensive. The smallest amount of smoke spreads with amazing rapidity'.

Lists of fires

In 2009, the government disclosed that there had been three fires which required external assistance since 1987:[21]

Date	Vessel	Location	Notes
17 February 1992	HMS Renown	Clyde	
30 April 1992	HMS Turbulent	Devonport	Explosion and fire in switchroom; 24 casualties from smoke
24 October 2003	HMS Trafalgar	Devonport	

In 2009, the government said there had been 20 medium scale fires (which were brought under control using ship's resources) since 1987.[22] These were defined as 'a localised fire such as a failure of mechanical equipment creating smoke and flame requiring use of significant onboard resources'.[23]

This parliamentary answer included one fire in 1984 and is shown on the next page along with a list of known fires on British nuclear submarines prior to 1987 is also available.[24]

▲ Fire on *HMS Astute*, Barrow, 18 April 2009

Date	Vessel	Location	Notes
10 December 1984	HMS Courageous	Alongside	
29 July 1987	HMS Sceptre	Not recorded	
26 August 1987	HMS Conqueror	Alongside	Engine room damage and burns casualties
15 November 1987	HMS Renown	Not recorded	
10 October 1988	HMS Renown	Clyde	
5 August 1989	HMS Valiant	Clyde	
22 December 1989	HMS Valiant	Alongside	
21 November 1991	HMS Trenchant	At sea	
3 November 1992	HMS Superb	At sea	
11 January 1993	HMS Tireless	At sea	
29 July 1993	HMS Revenge	At sea	
22 October 1993	HMS Tireless	Alongside	
7 April 1994	HMS Sovereign	Rosyth	
22 August 1995	HMS Sovereign	Rosyth	
16 October 1995	HMS Victorious	Alongside	
18 January 1999	HMS Talent	Devonport	
17 June 2001	HMS Sovereign	Clyde	
22 April 2002	HMS Victorious	At sea	
11 October 2006	HMS Vigilant	Clyde	
21 March 2007	HMS Tireless	At sea	Explosion and fire; Two fatalities

▼ Known fires on British nuclear submarines prior to 1987

Date	Submarine	Location	Notes
1963	Valiant	Barrow	Fire in reactor compartment while under construction
1965	Dreadnought	Rosyth	Fire in control room
September 1968	Valiant	Chatham	Two small fires

Date	Submarine	Location	Notes
August 1970	Resolution	Rosyth	Fire in control room
3 July 1972	Repulse	Rosyth	
January 1975	Repulse	Faslane	Fire from equipment overheating
July 1975	Courageous	Faslane	
1976/77	Repulse		Fire causing £200,000 damage
2 May 1976	Warspite	Liverpool	Major fire lasting 5 hours, 1 seriously injured and 4 others taken to hospital, 2 years to repair
March 1980	Revenge	Faslane	Electrical fire, jetty cable
18 September 1983	Conqueror	Devonport	
September 1985	Repulse	Rosyth	Fire on jetty heating system
1986	Splendid	Devonport	Fire in generator
26 August 1987	Conqueror	Devonport	Fire causing engine room damage and burns casualties

Between 1987 and April 2009 there were 213 small scale fires on British nuclear submarines.[25] By July 2014 this had risen to 243; of these 67 were on ballistic missile submarines (Polaris/ Trident).[26] This means that between April 2009 and July 2014 there was a fire on average once every six weeks. Between July 2012 and November 2014 there were a further 14 small scale fires on submarines.[27]

Collisions and Groundings
Collisions

McNeilly reports that details of the collision between HMS *Vanguard* and *Le Triomphant* in February 2009 are a closely guarded secret. He recounts that a Chief Petty Officer, who had been on *Vanguard* at the time of the crash, told him 'We thought, this is it, we're all going to die' and explained that the French submarine had taken a chunk out of the front of *Vanguard*, grazed down the side of the boat and dislodged High Pressure Air bottle groups. The Nuclear Information Service submitted a Freedom of Information request for reports of the collision. A heavily redacted version of several documents was released. This gives no indication of the circumstances or effect of the collision. It confirms that both submarines were on patrol at the time of the incident.

Excessive secrecy surrounding nuclear submarine collisions is not new. In 2013 a submariner described for the first time a collision between HMS *Warspite* and a Russian submarine in October 1968. Ian Wragg said 'There was an almighty bang and the boat rolled 360 degrees over. Nobody really knows why it happened, but most people feel that the Russian boat had slowed down and we ran into the back of it. We were all given a tot of rum.'[28] *Warspite* limped back to British waters and came into Lerwick with a damaged coning tower. Official reports said that the vessel had collided with an iceberg.

▲ HMS *Vanguard* entering Faslane at night after collision with *Le Triomphant*

Groundings

There have been a number of occasions in recent years when British nuclear submarines have run aground. Common features in these incidents have been a lack of navigation skills and poor communications.

On 19 November 2000, HMS *Triumph* ran aground off the West coast of Scotland. The submarine had just completed a five month deployment when the submarine was sent out again, from Devonport, on a submarine command training course. Because the original crew had already been at sea for so long 30% were replaced with personnel from other submarines.

The submarine was sailing towards the North Channel. They were approaching the continental shelf where the seabed rises to a depth of around 200m. A plan was prepared for the submarine to rise to 100m when they approached the shelf. The officers on duty did not use the automated Submarine Navigation and Processing System (SNAPS) properly. They also failed to make full use of the echo sounder to detect the rising seabed. As a result the submarine was 2.6 nautical miles away from its estimated position. The submarine hit the seabed at a depth of 200m and speed of 20 knots. Emergency Stations was piped. Then the main ballast tanks were blown and the submarine was brought to the surface. The Board of Inquiry concluded that

'The grounding was caused by poor navigation. Contributory factors included a widespread misunderstanding of SNAPS organisation and poor chartwork.'[29]

Ten days after this incident, on 29 November 2000, the Trident submarine HMS *Victorious* ran aground on Skelmorlie Bank in the Clyde estuary. As submarines depart from the Clyde a Towed Array Sonar system is attached by a long cable. HMS *Victorious* had planned to attach the Towed Array near Bute. However, when they approached Bute the wind was too strong. They decided to change course and go to the North of Cumbrae. When manoeuvring in this area a rope almost became tangled in the submarine's propulsor. So a third option was chosen. The submarine would sail to Loch Long and check the situation there. No clear plan was made for the move from Cumbrae to Loch Long. The Petty Officer who was logging the submarine's position was unaware that the submarine had increased speed to 10 knots. There was then an error in taking bearings to determine the vessel's position and the wrong course was selected. Skelmorlie bank is a sandbank in the Clyde estuary which is clearly marked with a large buoy. However, no-one on the submarine realised that they were sailing towards the wrong side of the buoy. They were 400 yards on the wrong side of it when the submarine grounded. At that point they were around 2.2km from the shore. Emergency Stations were sounded. The submarine then returned to Faslane. The Board of Inquiry concluded:

> 'The primary cause of the grounding was a failure of standard navigational practice and a lack of awareness amongst all members of the navigation team of the increased danger to safe navigation as soon as the submarine had deviated from its pre-briefed navigation plan.'[30]

On 6 November 2002, HMS *Trafalgar* ran aground on Fladda-Chuan, 6 kilometres north of Skye, while taking part in a submarine command course. Navigation aids had been deliberately concealed. This was done 'to increase the degree of navigational difficulty and hence pressure on the students'.[31] There was confusion on the submarine as to who was formally responsible for navigation. The trainee in control was using tracing paper which concealed some of the information on his chart. He did not properly take account of the significant tidal stream around Fladda-Chuain. As a result the submarine struck the bottom heavily at a speed of 14.7 knots. The Board of Inquiry concluded that HMS *Trafalgar* grounded because of human error. The Commanding Officer and the course teacher were both disciplined in a Court Martial. The inquiry report said 'Although a safety organisation was in place [on the submarine] and had worked effectively up until then, it failed to operate when most needed.'

The report said that there was 'good reason' for depriving the trainee commander of navigation aids and did not recommend that this practice should cease. Submarine Command Courses have continued to take place using nuclear submarines off the west coast of Scotland. The training deliberately places the trainees in difficult and confusing situations. The trainees control the submarine as they conduct a series of exercises, some of which are at high speed and close to other vessels.

On 26 May 2008, HMS *Superb* grounded on an underwater mountain in the Red Sea. A late decision was made to carry out the traverse at depth, without adequate attention to navigation. The Navigation Officer had failed to make full use of the two charts of the area which were available.[32] As a result of the damage, *Superb* was scrapped a few months after the incident.

On 22 October 2010, HMS *Astute* ran aground while conducting a boat transfer near the Isle of Skye. On three occasions the Officer of the Watch ignored instructions from other crew members to change course. It was several hours before the vessel could be refloated. During the attempt to dislodge the submarine it collided with the tug which was assisting it. The Board of Inquiry found,

'Preparations for, and conduct of the watch by the Officer of the Watch fell short of the standards required to maintain submarine safety. The planning for the boat transfer was insufficient to ensure safe completion and lacked appropriate command oversight'.

Communications between the bridge and the control room were poor. There were also problems communicating with MV *Omagh*, the vessel involved in the boat transfer. In 2009 the government published a list of 13 incidents where submarines had collided with other vessels or ran aground since 1988.[33] This can be supplemented by lists compiled by Scottish CND, reports of collisions with Russian submarines and other sources.[34, 35, 36]

▲ Left: HMS *Astute* aground on the Isle of Skye 22 October 2010
Right: HMS *Repulse* aground on the sand at Barrow after launch

▼ Combined list of known collisions

Date	Submarine	Location	Notes
October 1968	Warspite		Collision with Russian submarine, crew told to say they had hit an iceberg
7 October 1969	Renown	Kintyre	Collision with Irish MV Moyle while surfacing at night
1969	Revenge	Clyde	Collision with cattle boat while surfacing
January 1973	Repulse/ Revenge	Faslane	Collision while leaving dry dock, Repulse hydroplanes damaged
1981	Sceptre	Barents Sea	Collision with Russian submarine, crew told to say they had hit an iceberg
10 June 1985	Resolution	Florida	Collision while at US missile range
24 December 1986	Splendid		Collision with Russian submarine, towed array lost.
2 July 1988	Courageous	North Channel	Sank yacht Dalriada
November 1990	Trenchant	North of Arran	Sank Fishing Vessel Antares
13 May 2003	Tireless		Collision with iceberg in Marginal Ice Zone at depth of 60 metres.
4 February 2009	Vanguard		Collision with Le Triomphant, both submarines on patrol
22 October 2010	Astute	Skye	Collided with tug after running aground
April 2015	Talent		Collision with iceberg, £500,000 damage to coning tower.

▼ Occasions when British nuclear submarines are known to have run aground

Date	Submarine	Location	Notes
5 November 1967	Repulse	Barrow	Ran aground after launch
17 April 1971	Renown	Clyde	Hit sea bed in post refit trials, Captain court-martialled
13 October 1989	Spartan	Loch Linnhe	
March 1991	Valiant	North Norwegian Sea	
July 1996	Trafalgar	Off Isle of Skye	
July 1997	Trenchant	Off coast of Australia	
19 November 2000	Triumph	West coast of Scotland	Hit sea bed at depth of 200 m and speed of 20 knots
27 November 2000	Victorious	Clyde	Ran aground on Skelmorlie Bank
6 November 2002	Trafalgar	North of Skye	Hit seabed at 15 knots
26 May 2008	Superb	Red Sea	Hit underwater mountain. As a result the vessel was scrapped.
April 2009	Torbay	Eastern Mediterranean	
22 October 2010	Astute	Skye	Aground on Skye for several hours

Reactor Defects

McNeilly alludes to reactor problems which might result in reactors having to be replaced. This probably refers to the core cladding failure on the prototype submarine reactor at Dounreay in 2012. This incident was kept secret, including from the Dounreay Stakeholder Group, for over a year. The incident has a potential impact on all current British nuclear submarines. As a result of the problem, an additional nuclear refuelling has been arranged for HMS *Vanguard* and may be needed for HMS *Victorious*. This is only one of a series of major defects in the reactors on British nuclear submarines.

In 1989 cracking was discovered in the primary coolant circuit of the reactor on HMS *Warspite* during a refit. In January 1990, Scottish CND received a number of anonymous phone calls from someone working in Faslane. We were told 'there are cracks around the watery leg pipework in the primary circuits in the SGs [Steam Generators] in SSN and Polaris boats and they don't know how to fix them'. When asked how dangerous this was, the caller replied 'Let's just say we're talking about Chernobyl'. In a further call, we were told 'the emergency cooling system doesn't work at all. There was an incident at Faslane about two years ago when there was a near meltdown'. Hunter-killer submarines were initially confined to port, but Polaris submarines continued to be sent out on patrol. Checks were carried out on all nuclear submarines and several were scrapped as a result.[37]

On 12 May 2000, there was a leak of coolant from the reactor on HMS *Tireless* when the submarine was deployed in the Mediterranean. Experts in the UK wrongly advised the crew to restart the reactor, which made the problem worse. The vessel limped to Gibraltar where a year-long repair was carried out, promoting serious concerns from both the Spanish government and the authorities in Gibraltar. This was also a generic fault which could affect all submarines with PWR1 reactors. Checks and repairs were conducted over several years.

▲ HMS *Tireless* stranded in Gibraltar August 2000

Terrorism Risk

McNeilly was particularly concerned about the risk of a terrorist attack on a Trident submarine and the lack of adequate security arrangements, including the failure to check bags that were taken onboard by sailors and civilian staff.

The MOD treat the threat of a terrorist attack differently from the hazard of nuclear accident. One example is the Faslane Shiplift. Risk assessments for the shiplift show that if a large aircraft collides with the shiplift while there is an armed Trident submarine inside, then the building will collapse and all of the missiles will detonate, scattering lethal plutonium over a wide area. However, the accident assessment says that this risk is acceptable because the probability that an aircraft will accidentally fall out of the sky and land on this particular part of the earth is very remote. Common sense would suggest that the risk of a terrorist deliberately crashing an aircraft into the shiplift is much higher. The compliance criteria for the shiplift show that there is not a huge margin between the calculated risk of an aircraft accidentally causing the facility to collapse and the required safety criteria. This would suggest that the risk of a terrorist incident causing a nuclear accident at Faslane is unacceptably high.

Sabotage

McNeilly raises the prospect of deliberate sabotage of a Trident submarine by someone onboard. One example, which McNeilly quotes, of the potential for extreme behaviour on a nuclear submarine was the shooting dead of one officer and wounding of a second by a sailor on HMS *Astute* in Southampton in 2011. There are several examples of submarine sabotage from other parts of the world.

In 2001 Ernesto Cimminio, a Petty Officer in the US Navy, was charged with deliberately damaging more than 100 cables on the Trident submarine, USS *Alaska*.[38] Cimminio was abusing drugs at the time and having an affair with the wife of another sailor.[39] There were also reports that valves were deliberately shut when they shouldn't have been and that reactor control valves were cut on USS *San Juan* in 1996.[40]

The destruction of the Indian submarine INS *Sindhurakshak* in 2013 has been reported as likely to have been the result of sabotage. There was an explosion and fire which led to the detonation of torpedoes stored on the vessel. All 18 crew members who were onboard were killed.[41]

Uncontrolled dive

McNeilly says that there were problems with the diving planes on HMS *Victorious*. He said 'There were jokes about the fore-planes being defective throughout the entire submarine. They joked about getting them stuck in dive mode'. The diving planes on British nuclear submarines are critical. He also refers to problems with the diesel generators. A combination of reactor, diving plane and generator problems could be catastrophic on a submarine operating close to maximum depth.

On 9 April 1963 the USS *Thresher* was conducting trials when it went into an uncontrolled dive. The vessel sank to a depth of 2,600 metres and was lost with all 129 crew members. A Court of Inquiry concluded that the reactor had probably shut down, resulting in a loss of propulsion, and that the ballast system had also failed, possibly as a result of freezing temperatures.[42]

Today the US Navy has design principles to prevent a recurrence of this disaster. However, current British submarines fall short of these standards. This was revealed when the MOD failed to properly redact an electronic document issued to Scottish CND under the Freedom of Information Act.[43] The report from the Defence Nuclear Safety Regulator (DNSR) said that the reactors on British submarines are much less reliable that the reactors on American submarines. The hidden text in the document said:

> 'US established practice is to deliver a high reliability of propulsion, from the main propulsion system, even under reactor fault conditions. UK practice in current class submarines is to accept a much lower reliability from the main propulsion system, and to back this up with a very low power (but high reliability) emergency propulsion system. This system will not provide sufficient dynamic lift, so safety is achieved by procedural controls constraining the combinations of speed and depth, backed up by ballast systems (but this may not be effective under all circumstances).'[44]

This means that, whereas safety is engineered into US submarines, on British submarines safety is based on personnel following procedures. The DNSR report revealed that, when compared with US standards, 'it is clear that the UK programme currently falls short of current relevant good practice.'[45]

A British submarine faced with a loss of power at close to maximum depth could be placed in an uncontrolled dive without the means of regaining the surface. McNeilly recounts an incident on HMS *Vanguard* when the submarine was 'extremely close to being lost'. This is almost certainly a reference to a near disaster on the submarine when operating in the Celtic Deep at close to maximum depth in July 1998. A sailor contacted the *Sunday Mail* and told them 'The boat was shuddering and shaking. We were on our knees praying. Everyone was scared out of their wits because we had never experienced anything like this'.[46]

Apparently, the reactor on HMS *Vanguard* had shut down. The crew tried to get a back-up power system going but it failed to work. By this time the submarine was descending rapidly in a deep dive. The vessel was eventually brought back under control when the reactor started up again. John Large, a nuclear engineer, said 'This is an extremely serious problem for this class of submarine. It's horrific – the worst nightmare.' The Royal Navy admitted that HMS *Vanguard* had been forced to make 'an unscheduled surface during a training exercise', but denied that there was any cause for concern.

Notes

1. http://www.robedwards.com/2015/05/trident-is-a-disaster-waiting-to-happensays-nuclear-whistleblower.html
2. http://robedwards.typepad.com/files/the-nuclear-secrets.pdf
3. ibid
4. The photo shows two sailors on top of each other. McNeilly says the UK wasn't following this practice.
5. MOD annual report and accounts 2013/14
6. https://ricochet.com/archives/sleep-when-youre-dead/
7. https://www.gov.uk/government/uploads/system/uploads/attachment_data/file/407154/20150122-DNSR-Annual-Report-2013-14-Issue-FINAL.pdf
8. http://robedwards.typepad.com/files/shefannual-report-0809.pdf
9. Board of Inquiry into the grounding of HMS *Astute* 22 October 2010
10. ibid
11. Board of Inquiry Grounding of HMS *Triumph* on 19 November 2000
12. Board of Inquiry into the collision of HMS *Tireless* on 13 May 2003, Faslane Flotilla, 5 June 2003.
13. RNAD Coulport Jetty Missile Loading Incident 3 December 1987 Report of the Board of Inquiry, 14 December 1987.
14. Report of the Chief Inspector of Marine Accidents into the collision between the Fishing Vessel *Antares* and HMS *Trenchant* with the loss of four lives on 22 November 1990.
15. Board of Inquiry into the collision of HMS *Tireless* on 13 May 03, Faslane Flotilla, 5 June 2003.
16. *Diaries: In power 1983-1992*, Alan Clark
17. http://www.crs-csex.forces.gc.ca/boi-ce/rp/hmcs-ncsm/rp/index-eng.aspx
18. Board of Inquiry into the circumstances surrounding the deaths of LOM(WSM) Paul David McCann D252555M and OM(WSM)2 Anthony Huntrod D261007R and the injury to xxxx of HMS *Tireless* on 20 March 2007
19/20. ibid
21/22. Hansard 16 September 2009 Col 2223W
23. Hansard 2 April 2009
24. Cracking Under Pressure, Scottish CND & Faslane Peace Camp 1992
25. Hansard 2 April 2009
26. Hansard 3 July 2012
27. Hansard 3 December 2014
28. http://www.chad.co.uk/news/local/ian-relives-nuclear-sub-crash-terror-1-6149498
29. Board of Inquiry – Grounding of HMS *Triumph* on 19 November 2000
30 Board of Inquiry into the circumstances surrounding the grounding of HMS *Victorious* on Skelmorlie Bank on 29 November 2000

31. Board of Inquiry into the Grounding of HMS *Trafalgar* on Fladda-Chuain on 6 November 2002, HMS *Montrose*, 12 November 2002

32. Board of Inquiry report into the circumstances surrounding the grounding of HMS *Superb* on 26 May 2008

33. http://www.publications.parliament.uk/pa/cm200809/cmhansrd/cm090402/text/90402w0024.htm09040272000014

34/35/36/37. Cracking Under Pressure, Scottish CND

38. http://web.kitsapsun.com/archive/2001/06-02/0006_uss_alaska_damage__navy_drops_sab.html

39. http://www.seattleweekly.com/2001-02-28/news/slicing-the-sub/

40. https://news.google.com/newspapers?nid=1915&dat=19971008&id=MZdGAAAAIBAJ&sjid=evgMAAAAIBAJ&pg=2083,1506820&hl=en

41. http://www.sunday-guardian.com/news/submarine-fire-may-have-beensabotage

42. Navy News 26 October 1993

43. http://www.banthebomb.org/images/stories/pdfs/substandardsubmarines.pdf

44/45. Successor SSBN – safety regulator's advice on the selection of the propulsion plant in support of the future deterrent review note. DNSR, 4 November 2009.

46. http://www.banthebomb.org/archives/magazine/nfs989o.htm

If Britain fired Trident

The humanitarian consequences of a nuclear attack by a Trident submarine on Moscow

John Ainslie

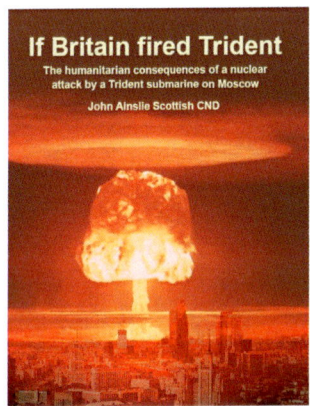

These excerpts are taken from the full report, first published by Scottish CND in February 2013.

Summary

Destruction of the Russian capital has been at the centre of British nuclear planning for 50 years. The current plan for a like-for-like replacement for Trident suggests that the Ministry of Defence still regards this as the key damage criteria. This report explains what "flattening Moscow" would mean for the 11.5 million residents of Europe's second largest city.[1]

This study gives an illustration of the catastrophic humanitarian consequences of an attack on a large urban area with multiple nuclear weapons. It also shows that the devastation would be on such a scale that humanitarian and emergency response agencies would be unable to provide an adequate response.[2]

The targeting policy for Trident was established in the early 1980s. The primary aim-points were to be specific locations within the city of Moscow and command bunkers in the surrounding area. Today an attack on these targets with 40 nuclear warheads, the normal complement on a Trident submarine, would result in 5.4 million deaths, 4.5 million inside the city and a further 870,000 in the Moscow Region. This is an estimate of casualties within the first few months and does not take account of long-term effects.[3]

In estimating the number of casualties, the starting point was to consider the effect of blast damage from each explosion. Blasts alone would kill almost everyone within 1 kilometre of each target, plus a large proportion of residents who were between 1 and 2 kilometres of each site. Heat and immediate nuclear radiation would be additional risks to residents within 2.2

kilometres of each explosion. Those with severe burns or blast injuries would be less likely to survive large doses of radiation. This would result in high mortality rates within these areas. Some residents would be shielded from heat and gamma radiation by adjacent buildings, but those in skyscrapers would be particularly vulnerable. Today Moscow has many of the tallest buildings in Europe.

Fire would be a major killer in any nuclear attack on an urban area. The intense heat from the fireball would start fires near each explosion. Beyond 3 kilometres from each Ground Zero, fires would be triggered by blast damage to gas and electrical fittings rather than heat. The blast wave can extinguish flames, but it can also cause fire to spread more rapidly between buildings. Within 3 kilometres of each explosion it is unlikely that residents would be able to prevent fires from expanding. Many of the city's power stations would be set alight. Individual fires would grow and could combine into a destructive firestorm which would create hurricane-force winds, burn up almost all combustible material and asphyxiate large numbers of residents.

The nuclear weapons would be detonated as ground-burst rather than air-burst explosions, in order to destroy underground command centres. Ground-burst explosions create vast quantities of radioactive fallout. Fallout from the explosions within Moscow would be lethal to many residents of the city and its suburbs. The attacks on command bunkers outside the city would spread more radiation over a wide area. Many houses in the suburbs would provide little protection from nuclear fallout. Most buildings in the city could reduce the dose from fallout, if intact. But in many cases they would be badly damaged and would provide little protection. The interaction between fire and fallout would increase the number of fatalities within Moscow. Fires would force residents to flee from shelter and to move in the open, where they would be more exposed to radiation from fallout. In some cases people would flee into areas where the radiation levels were higher.

Fatality rates would be around 95% within 1.6 kilometres of each explosion and at greater distances directly downwind, due to fallout. There would be extensive fires within 3 kilometres of each Ground Zero. Fires would be a particular problem in areas which lay between two or more explosions. Most of the city and large parts of Moscow Region would be affected by high levels of radiation from fallout.

The casualties would include doctors, nurses and patients in hospitals across the city. Several of Moscow's largest hospitals would be completely destroyed and others would be seriously damaged. It would be difficult to bring aid and assistance to a city contaminated with radioactive fallout. The scope for providing humanitarian assistance to the huge number of victims would be very limited. Schools across the city would be flattened or torn apart. Over 788,000 of those killed would be under 18 years old.

If there was warning and residents took shelter in underground bunkers and the subway then the number of fatalities would be lower. However, it is likely that thousands of people would try to flee the city. If the attack took place while they were travelling or sheltering in the suburbs, then the reduction in casualties would be less significant. If there was a firestorm then many of those in shelters would die from carbon monoxide poisoning. In 1978 the UK government concluded that if warheads were detonated as groundburst explosions, the resulting fallout would reduce the effectiveness of Russian civil defence plans.

There would be more fatalities in an attack from two submarines and fewer if some warheads were intercepted by Russian Anti Ballistic Missiles. The scenario assumes average wind speed and direction. In some weather conditions casualty numbers would be higher.

Attack scenario

British nuclear targeting

The essence of British nuclear targeting today has been revealed. In October 2012 then Deputy Prime Minister, Nick Clegg, said:

> "The idea of a like-for-like entirely unchanged replacement of Trident is basically saying we will spend billions and billions and billions of pounds on a nuclear missile system designed with the sole strategic purpose of flattening Moscow at the press of a button".[5]

This followed an earlier comment from Nick Harvey, former Armed Forces minister, that the Ministry of Defence (MOD) was locked in a 1980s mindset of having nuclear weapons to "flatten Moscow". Harvey had been leading a major review of nuclear alternatives, which included a fresh look at the rationale behind the British nuclear force.

When Sir Menzies Campbell wrote in the *Financial Times* that it was time for Britain to abandon the "Moscow Criterion", there was a reply from three men who had been closely involved in the Trident programme at the highest level. Sir David Omand, Sir Kevin Tebbit and Franklin Miller KBE argued that a serious confrontation with Russia was not unthinkable. They said that Britain's possession of nuclear weapons was based on "holding at risk what any potential adversary's leadership would value most" and added "in the Russian case, Moscow has, of course, always represented the very centre of state power".[6]

It is reasonable to conclude that the primary targeting of the British Trident force today is against Moscow. Declassified papers in The National Archive provide an insight into what this means.[7] The term "Moscow criterion" was initially used, in 1962, for the targeting of the capital and the next four largest cities in the Soviet Union. Polaris missiles were to cause "breakdown" level damage in each city. Until 1979 breakdown was defined as causing severe structural damage to 50% of the buildings in a city, resulting in around 50% fatalities. In 1979 the threshold was lowered to 40%.

A review of nuclear policy in 1972 noted that the Soviets had built underground command centres outside the capital. But there was no serious attempt to target the bunkers at this time, because this was beyond the capability of Polaris. In 1978 the Callaghan government considered replacing Polaris. Officials drew up the Duff-Mason report. This presented three damage criteria. One account says that Option 1 was "to destroy the command centres of the Soviet political and military systems (both above and below ground) inside the Moscow ring road and extra ones in the wider Moscow area".[8] However, the emphasis was probably on disrupting rather than destroying the command system.[9]

British intelligence calculated that there were 27 ex-urban national command bunkers, concentrated at eight sites.[10] The Duff-Mason report was adopted and amended by the Thatcher Government who decided, in December 1979, to acquire the Trident C4 missile system. In a presentation to the MISC 7 committee, Defence Minister Francis Pym argued that the primary focus should be on Moscow, but he added that the force should also have some capability to attack some of the command bunkers.[11] In January 1982 the MISC 7 committee decided that Britain should acquire Trident D5 rather than Trident C4. While this change was largely to retain compatibility with the US Navy, a secondary advantage was that D5 would be more effective against command bunkers.[12]

In 1981 the MOD carried out a review of Strategic Targeting Policy, looking ahead to Trident. This reaffirmed that Moscow was the main focus. While the report itself remains classified, comments on the draft policy suggest what it may have said. Group Captain Miller prepared a briefing for the Chief of Air Staff in which he noted: "With the improved accuracy of the new system we should plan to attack specific key areas rather than built up areas as a whole."[13] Admiral Leach, Chief of Naval

Staff, used the term "Moscow plus hardened bunkers."[14] There was a departure from the previous "breakdown" approach of achieving a prescribed level of destruction across a city. Targeting command bunkers was a feature of the new policy.

There was further confirmation of the focus on bunkers in 1995 when Field Marshall Nigel Bagnall, former Chief of General Staff, was asked about the targeting of Trident. He said, "It is more than just the destruction of Moscow, it is the destruction of their command and control system".[15]

It is possible to deduce that Britain's primary nuclear policy today is to target Moscow. Warheads are probably targeted on particular facilities, including command centres within the city and at the main bunkers outside the capital. The MOD are currently upgrading the Trident warhead to a new Mk4A specification. The Mk4A will be substantially more effective than the original Mk4 against command bunkers.

Defence ministers are fond of saying that Trident missiles are now "de-targeted", but the significance of this should not be exaggerated. In 1994 Britain, the US and Russia agreed that their missiles would not normally hold real target data. This was to reduce the risk that the accidental launch of a single missile could trigger nuclear war. It does not mean that Britain has no target plans. It is almost certain that the Trident submarine on patrol carries electronic plans which can be implemented if the Captain receives authorisation.

Model target list

A target list has been created in order to illustrate the effect of an attack by 40 warheads from one Trident submarine. The government of Russia is heavily concentrated in the central district of Moscow. This is also the location of several underground command bunkers. This list assumes that 10 warheads are targeted on facilities in the city centre, a further 10 elsewhere in the city and 20 at command bunkers outside the city, but within Moscow region. The centre of Moscow is likely to be completely destroyed, regardless of the precise targets in the central district. The identification of individual targets across the city may not be accurate, but the list provides a reasonable basis for estimating the overall effect on Moscow as a whole.

Assumptions

The calculations below assume that the wind is from the Southwest, with a windspeed of 7 metres per second. These are typical wind conditions. Visibility is assumed to be 40 km.[16] The population are at their normal place of residence and there is no notice of the attack. The potential for

Target	Location	Missile/Warhead
Special Communications HQ	Bolshoy Kiselni Lane	2.1
Presidential Administration	Old Square	2.2
Communications Ministry	Tverskaya Street	2.3
Kremlin		2.4
Defence Ministry	Znamenka Street	2.5
Navy Headquarters	Bolshoy Koslowski Lane	3.1
Moscow District HQ	Kosmondamianskaya Embankment	3.2
Ground Forces HQ	Frunzenskaya Embankment	3.3
Rear/Logistics HQ	Bolshoya Pirogovskaya Street	3.4
White House		3.5

▲ Table 1. Ten Targets in Moscow city centre

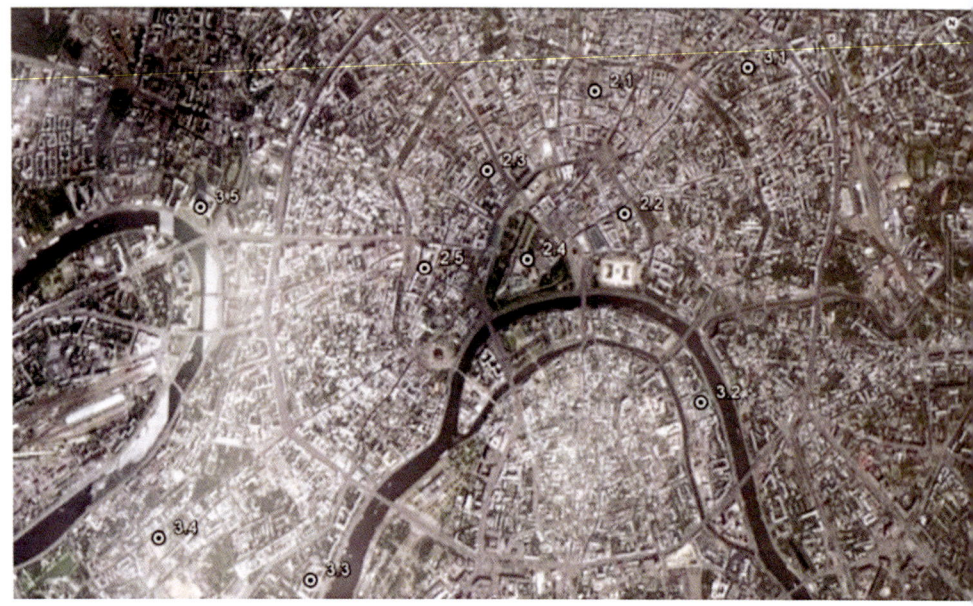

▲ Chart 1. Ten Targets in Moscow city centre

taking shelter in civil defence bunkers and the subway is considered towards the end of the report, as is the impact of different weather conditions. Calculations are based on the 2010 Russian census. The geographical boundaries of Moscow which were in place in 2010 are used throughout this report.

Effects

Three consequences of a nuclear explosion (blast, heat and initial radiation) are often grouped together as prompt effects, as distinct from radioactive fallout which is a long-term hazard. However, this grouping may not adequately address the issue of fire. Blast and initial radiation are effective within one minute of the explosion. Direct burns from thermal radiation are also experienced within this timescale. Fires can be initiated by heat from the fireball and as a result of blast damage. The intensity of fires is likely to increase over the first hour and the resulting conflagrations can remain a major hazard for several hours. Fires may have a critical effect in determining how people behave. In order to escape flames and smoke, residents may move away from shelter and into areas where they are at greater risk from fallout.

Two effects modelling programmes in the public domain are Weapons Effects (Version 2.1 December 1984) and Hotspot (Version 2.07.2 August 2011).[17] Weapon Effects was produced by Horizon Technology for the Defense Nuclear Agency and was originally classified. Hotspot was produced by Lawrence Livermore National Laboratory to model the effects of nuclear accidents. It includes a nuclear explosion model. A comparison of the programmes, Table 4, shows that Weapon Effects gives slightly higher estimates for blast, but significantly lower estimates for heat and initial radiation. Hotspot was used as the primary source for this paper.

Blast effects within 3 kilometres of each Ground Zero
Within 500 metres of each explosion the blast overpressure would be 97 psi. This would completely destroy all buildings. This effect would be particularly noticeable in the middle of Moscow, where there would be five explosions, 1 kilometre or less apart. At 500 metres, the direct blast effect on the body would be fatal for 100% of those who were exposed to it, before taking account of falling buildings, heat and radiation.

Between 500 metres and 1 kilometre, rubble would be thrown a considerable distance from each building. In the Mill Race experiment a building was subjected to 30 psi in a US nuclear test. Masonry from the front and side walls was discovered 60 metres from the site.[18] Within 1 kilometre of each explosion the blast overpressure would be 20 psi. This would destroy or severely damage even the most substantially built reinforced-concrete buildings in the city. Injuries sustained from collapsed buildings would result in a fatality level from blast alone of around 100%.[19]

At 1.5 kilometres the overpressure would be just under 10 psi. This would severely damage or destroy many reinforced concrete buildings. One recent report indicates that most buildings would be destroyed by overpressure values of between 10 and 12 psi.[20] The percentage of fatalities from blast damage would decline from 100% at 1 kilometre to 58% at 1.5 kilometres. Almost all who survived in this area would be injured.

Reinforced concrete buildings would suffer significant damage at distances of between 1.5 and 1.8 kilometres (6-9 psi). Steel framed buildings would be seriously damaged between 1.7 and 2.4 kilometres (4-7 psi).[21] Wood-framed buildings would collapse at just over 2 kilometres from Ground Zero (5 psi). At 2 kilometres, the effects of blast would kill 13% of residents and injure around 54%.

Someone standing up in a standard house 2.6 kilometres (3.5 psi) from Ground Zero would be at 50% risk of death from damage to the building.[22] If they were lying down then they would be at a similar risk of death from blast damage if they were 1.7 kilometres (7 psi) from Ground Zero. At 2.8 kilometres (3 psi) the wind speed would be 152 kph (95 mph).[23]

Effects of initial radiation and direct burns
at between 1 and 2.2 kilometres from each Ground Zero
Residents would be exposed to two forms of direct radiation. The main hazard would be gamma radiation, but neutron radiation would also contribute to the total dose. Initial radiation would affect residents before most buildings were destroyed by blast.

Many residents would not be within line-of-sight of the fireball because of shielding from buildings. Within the first second of the explosion, the fireball would expand and rise. As it rises, the gamma radiation would be emitted from higher above the ground. The shielding effect from buildings would decline. Meanwhile, the amount of gamma radiation emitted from the fireball would reduce. Between 0.1 seconds after the explosion and 1 second after the explosion it will have declined by a factor of 10.[24]

Between 1 and 2 kilometres from Ground Zero many people would be killed, and others would be injured, by blast damage. The radiation dose which would be fatal for injured residents would be lower than that for healthy adults. The combination of exposure to initial radiation and blast injury would have a significant effect on mortality between 1.4 and 2.2 kilometres from Ground Zero. Severe burns combined with radiation exposure would be fatal for all those exposed within these distances. The risk to residents in high-rise buildings would be higher, because the proportion in direct line-of-sight with the fireball would be greater.

Fire
The development of fires in the aftermath of a nuclear explosion is a key issue for several reasons. In some circumstances, such as at Hiroshima, fire can be the biggest killer. Fire can also have a major impact on how people behave, including their ability to remain in shelter and their exposure to

radioactive fallout. Thirdly, extensive fire damage is an underlying assumption behind models which estimate the global impact of multiple nuclear explosions on the climate. Research into how fires develop after a nuclear explosion, including the relationship between fire and blast, was carried out in the United States in the late 1970s and early 1980s. Some of this work was to inform civil defence planning. The possibility of deliberately using fire from nuclear explosions as a way of inflicting maximum damage to cities was also explored. Table 2 shows the distance at which materials may ignite if in line-of-sight of a 100 kiloton nuclear fireball.[25]

Distance from Ground Zero (kms)	Thermal Radiation (cal/cm^2)	Material which ignites
2.1	24	90% probability of igniting interior furnishing
2.6	16	50% probability of igniting interior furnishing
3.1	11	Cotton
3.4	9	Some polyester fabrics
3.5	8	10% probability of igniting interior furnishing
4 - 4.8	4-6	Newspaper

▲ Table 2. Ignition of material relative to distance from Ground Zero

A paper written in 2007 examines the thermal effects of a groundburst 10 kiloton explosion in a city. It illustrates how heat is distributed in three dimensions.[26] Areas behind tall buildings would be less hot because they are shielded from thermal radiation. As the fireball rises, these cooler areas shrink. For a 100-kiloton explosion, the peak emission of thermal radiation is 0.3 seconds after the weapon detonates. 50% of the heat is emitted by 0.5 seconds after detonation and 90% is emitted by 2.2 seconds after detonation.[27] During this period the fireball is expanding and rising. If the Mk4A Trident warhead is fused for near-surface-burst detonation, with a Height of Burst below 250 metres, then the Height of Burst should be added to these figures. In this case the shielding effect will be less.

In the case of a 1 Megaton explosion, the blast wave is 800 metres from Ground Zero 1.8 seconds after detonation. It is 4.8 kilometres from Ground Zero after 11 seconds and 6.4 kilometres from Ground Zero after 16 seconds. So, at 6.4 kilometres there would be a gap of 15 seconds between the pulse of thermal radiation and the arrival of the shock wave.[28] These figures suggest that the heat/blast interval at 2 kilometres would be 4 seconds and at 3 kilometres, 6 seconds, for a 1 Megaton explosion. The intervals for a 100 kiloton explosion would be longer. The intervals are unlikely to be long enough to allow a full-scale fire to develop, but, where thermal radiation is above 20 cal/cm^2, there could be almost instantaneous combustion of a significant proportion of the material in a room.

When the blast wave arrives it has a complex effect on the development of fires. The blast wave can extinguish flames. However, some US tests indicated that blast overpressures of 5 psi and less did not have this effect.[29] In addition, where the blast wave does suppress initial flames the material may later reignite.[30]

The blast wave would also eject combustible material from apartments into streets and gardens. There would be a substantial build up of debris, some of it readily combustible, in open areas. As a result, although the blast wave would reduce the number of buildings in which thermally-induced fires were developing, it would increase the ease with which fire would spread between buildings. Even Moscow's widest thoroughfares would cease to provide effective firebreaks, because they would be filled with smouldering debris.

The blast wave would also initiate secondary fires. Gas pipes would be ruptured when heaters and cookers were blown away. Blast damage would also trigger electrical fires. Where overpressure was around 2 psi most fires would be caused by blast rather than thermal radiation.[31] This would result in sustained fires in 2% of buildings which were 3.5 kilometres from a 100 kiloton explosion.[32] Some secondary fires would be ignited as far as 8.8 kilometres from the explosion, where the overpressure was greater than 0.5 psi.[33] Brode described how the risk of fire depends on the strength of the building and the flammability of its contents. Overpressure of 0.5 psi would cause fires in lightly constructed buildings containing highly flammable material.[34]

The interaction between blast and fire becomes even more complex when there are several nuclear explosions. A 1979 report into blast/fire interaction said, "The extension of fire-start (and fire spread) models to a multi-burst case appears to be a rather complex project involving many poorly defined phenomena".[35]

The targeting scenario described assumes that there are only very small time intervals between each explosion. In many cases this would mean that a building was exposed to thermal radiation from several explosions and then the blast waves each of the detonations. The proportion of the building that was ignited would be increased because it would be exposed to thermal radiation from several directions and the shielding effect would be reduced. However, the time interval between thermal radiation from later explosions and the first blast wave would be shorter, reducing the time that some fires would have to develop. The amount of debris that was ejected into the streets would be greater.

In some cases, buildings would be subjected to the blast wave from one explosion before they were exposed to thermal radiation from a second explosion. The interior space of buildings would be more exposed to heat because of blast damage. A higher proportion of fires would develop in this situation.[36]

In the immediate vicinity of the fireball a large amount of material is incinerated. Other combustible material may then be buried beneath piles of masonry. It has been suggested that, after the initial effects have subsided, there may be fewer fires in this central area, and more in a ring or doughnut around it.[37] There may be a higher risk of fire where buildings have been damaged rather than completely destroyed.[38]

Ten 100-kiloton explosions close together may have a similar effect, in terms of displacing the fire area, to a single one megaton explosion. This could mean that fire is likely to be concentrated in a doughnut around the edge of central district, rather than in the vicinity of the Kremlin. The fire risk may also be higher than otherwise expected in areas which lie between the devastated central district and individual explosions elsewhere in the city. For example, there might be extensive fires to the North of central district, as a result of the combined effect of a series of explosions.

The ability of the local population to bring fires under control would have a major effect on the spread and intensity of fires. The scale and extent of devastation resulting from a multi-warhead attack on Moscow would be such that fire-fighting efforts are likely to be very limited. Water supplies would be disrupted, roads blocked and fire engines damaged and destroyed. Within the 2 psi blast zone (3.5 kilometres) sporadic fires could develop if they were not tackled within 30 minutes and this could lead to extensive fires.[39]

Residents who were already injured by falling masonry and debris would be less likely to survive if they were also victims of fire.[40] In addition, those who were suffering from burns and smoke inhalation would succumb to lower levels of radiation than residents who were uninjured.

Where a large number of substantial fires take hold at the same time, there is a risk that a firestorm may develop. A firestorm develops its own momentum. Hurricane-force winds of 120 kph (75 mph) are created around the firestorm, sucking in air from all directions.[41] The temperature in the firestorm rises and a large proportion of combustible material is burnt. Residents above ground would not survive the intense heat. Those in shelters are likely to die from carbon monoxide poisoning, unless their shelter had a functioning independent air supply system.[42] They might also be exposed to extreme heat. One account of the bombing of Dresden describes the basements and shelter as "both crematoria and gas chambers combined."[43] Postol argued that the number of fatalities could increase by a factor of 2.5 where there was a firestorm.[44]

In a multiple-warhead attack on Moscow it is possible that two or more firestorms may develop. In this situation it is possible that two firestorms of different size may combine and consume an area which is up to 50% greater than the sum of the areas of the two firestorms.[45]

The development of firestorms and the combination of multiple firestorms are both dependent on weather conditions, including wind speed and stability. Analysis of Second World War fire raids suggests that rain and humidity has less effect than might be expected.

Radioactive fallout

The greatest problem from fallout will be from radioactive dust from the 10 nuclear explosions in the central district. This will be a major hazard downwind of this area. In addition there will be fallout from each of the other explosions in the city. Fallout from some of the explosions at bunkers outside Moscow is likely to reach the city. If the wind is from the Southwest the main problem would be fallout from Odintsovo-10. This would affect the North of the city. Fallout from bunkers would be a greater problem if the wind was from the South or South-Southwest, because this would blow fallout from the multiple explosions around Chekhov towards Moscow.

Table 3 shows how the effective radiation dose would increase over time in the case of someone who remained in the open directly downwind at 2, 5 and 10 kilometres from a 100 kiloton explosion.

Period of time	Effective dose (Sieverts)		
	2 km	5 km	10 km
1 hour	81	47	25
6 hours	120	84	61
24 hours	140	100	82
4 days	150	120	97
1 year	180	150	120

▲ Table 3. Build up of effective dose over time

The number of casualties is affected by the degree of protection provided by buildings or other shelter. There is a significant difference between the design of buildings in Moscow and most of the structures outside the city. In the suburbs there are a large number of one and two storey houses, whereas most of the residential properties in the city are apartment blocks. There are also many dachas, summer cottages, outside the city.

Many of the buildings in Moscow would, if intact, provide significant protection from fallout. However, damage from blast and fire would greatly reduce the protection they would provide.[46] Most of the properties outside the capital would provide less protection. Although these houses would be far less affected by blast and heat, they would have little effect in reducing the dose from fallout. One storey houses have a Protective Factor of 2 or 3. The apartments in blocks of flats have Protective Factors between 10 and 50. Basements in houses have a Protective Factor of 10. Underground parts of large buildings can have a Protective Factor of 100 or more. The Protection Factor for those in the open is 1.

Table 4 shows short-term mortality rates, within two months, in specific fallout zones. In the case of the most highly contaminated areas the criteria adopted were the effective dose over 1 and 6 hours. The casualty estimates are all based on the total effective dose over 4 days, taking account of the protection factors and the mortality rates.

Fallout zone	Urban area Damaged	Urban area Undamaged	Suburbs Undamaged
1hr dose 30-50 Sv	0.94		
1hr dose 5-30 Sv	0.63		
6hr dose 10-50 Sv		0.55	0.95
4 day dose 10-20 Sv	0.6	0.34	0.73
4 day dose 5-10 Sv	0.26	0.13	0.3
4 day dose 1-5 Sv	0.07	0.03	0.06

▲ Table 4. Mortality rates associated with fallout zones

For those in damaged areas of Moscow where residents received an effective dose of 30-50 Sv within the first hour, this would itself result in a mortality rate of 0.75. This would rise to 0.94 with the total dose after 4 days. Where the one hour dose was 5-30 Sv, the one-hour mortality rate of 0.42 would rise to 0.63 with the 4-days dose. In suburbs where the dose was 10-50 Sv after six hours, the mortality rate from this dose would be 0.88 rising to 0.95 with the 4-day dose.

Some residents are likely to move location during this initial 4-day period. Where they are in a room which provided a Protective Factor of 10 or more, then their 4-day dose is likely to be higher if they have to spend up to 24 hours in the open in order to reach an area with significantly less radiation. Where they have limited shelter, Protective Factor of 1 or 2, then their 4-day dose may be lower if they take similar action. It is assumed that the overall effect on the whole population might remain the same as if everyone remained where they were.

One recent study concludes that residents should remain in the best available shelter for at least 12 hours when there is a single low-yield explosion in an urban area.⁴⁷ This issue will be more complex when there is extensive radioactive contamination over a wide area from 40 surface burst 100-kiloton explosions.

Notes

1. The only city in Europe which is larger than Moscow is Istanbul.

2. The Red Cross have highlighted the "lack of any adequate humanitarian response capacity" to a nuclear explosion. Working towards the elimination of nuclear weapons, Council of delegates of the international red cross and red crescent movement, 26 November 2011,

3. Philip Webber outlines the potential long-term environmental impact of a UK Trident attack in "Could One Trident Submarine Cause Nuclear Winter", SGR, 2008,

4. http://www.bbc.co.uk/news/uk-politics-20116648

5. http://www.guardian.co.uk/uk/2012/sep/26/trident-nuclear-missiles-review-downgrading

6. UK cannot afford to be complacent. Letter from Sir David Omand, Sir Kevin Tebbit and Mr Franklin Miller to the Financial Times, 22 May 2012.

7. This archive evidence is explored in detail in Unacceptable Damage, John Ainslie, Scottish CND, February 2013.

8. Cabinets and the Bomb, Peter Hennessey, OUP, 2007, page 324.

9. "disruption of the main governmental organs of the Soviet state" Factors Relating to Further Consideration of the Future of the United Kingdom Nuclear Deterrent (Duff-Mason report), Part II Criteria for Deterrence, Summary, The National Archive (TNA) DEFE 19-275 e1 para 2

10. Duff-Mason report, Part II Annex A: Unacceptable Damage, 30 November 1978, TNA DEFE 25-335.

11. Speaking note for Secretary of State for MISC 7 meeting on 5 November 1979, TNA DEFE 13-752 e1. Due to a date error this paper was in a file covering 1970. If it had been in the correct file the document might have been redacted. 12 The MOD calculated that One warhead from a D5 missile would have a similar effect on a bunker as four warheads from a C4 missile, because D5 was more accurate.

12. Kmz file: Google Earth:

13. "Brief for Chief of Air Staff for presentation to SofS on strategic nuclear targeting, Group Captain Miller, 23 October 1981, TNA AIR 8-2846 e67ii

14. In a critique of the new targeting policy, Leach said that "Moscow plus hardened bunkers" had not been the planning assumption when the initial Trident C4 decision had been taken. His comment implies that it was part of the new approach. British Strategic Nuclear Targeting Policy, Assistant Secretary CNS, 21 October 1981, TNA AIR8-2846 e66

15. Moscow Criterion, BBC, broadcast July 1995

16. Hotspot provides three visibility options: 20, 40 and 80 kms.

17. Weapon Effects: Hotspot:

18. Structural Debris Experiments at Operation Mill Race, JR Rempel et al. Asilomar conference 1983.

19. Vulnerability of populations and the urban health care systems to nuclear weapon attack – examples for four American cities. WC Bell & CE Dallas, 2007, page 13.

20. A study on nuclear blast overpressure on buildings and other infrastructures using Geospatial Technology. C Vijayaraghavan et al. 2012

21. A study on nuclear blast overpressure on buildings and other infrastructures using Geospatial Technology.

22. The Effects of Nuclear War, Office of Technology Assessment, May 1979. p 19

23. The Effects of Nuclear War, Office of Technology Assessment, May 1979.

24. Effects of Nuclear Weapons, Glasstone, p328.

25. Effects of Nuclear Weapons, Glasstone, p289; Fire and Strategic Targeting, Brode, p13.

26. Thermal radiation from nuclear detonations in urban environments, RE Marrs, WC Moss & B Whitlock, Lawrence Livermore National Laboratory, June 2007.

27. Thermal radiation from nuclear detonations in urban environments, p 3

28. Possible fatalities from superfires, T Postol, Medical Implications of Nuclear War, 1986, p 18f.

29. Blast/Fire interactions, Program Formulation, Defense Civil Preparedness Agency, 1979, p A-1239

30. Fire and the related effects of nuclear explosions, Proceedings of the 1982 Asilomar Conference, Federal Emergency Management Agency. p VI-5

31. Fire and the related effects of nuclear explosions, Proceedings of the 1982 Asilomar Conference, p III-11

32. Blast/Fire interactions, Program Formulation, Defense Civil Preparedness Agency, 1979, p A-4

33. Fire and the related effects of nuclear explosions, Proceedings of the 1982 Asilomar Conference, p VI-13

34. Fire damage and strategic targeting, Harold L Brode, Defence Nuclear Agency, 1984, p 24.

35. Blast/Fire interactions, Program Formulation, Defense Civil Preparedness Agency, 1979, p 11

36. Assessment of combined effects of blast and fire on personnel survivability, Federal Emergency Management Agency, 1982.

37. If a firestorm is established it is expected to move into the heavily-destroyed centre of the doughnut after it takes hold. Proceedings of the 17th Asilomar Conference on Fire and Blast Effects of Nuclear Weapons, 1983, p 83.

38. Assessment of combined effects of blast and fire on personnel survivability, Federal Emergency Management Agency, 1982.

39. Evaluation of the nuclear fire threat to urban areas, SJ Wierama, Defense Civil Preparedness Agency, 1973, p 6.

40. Possible fatalities from superfires, T Postol, Medical Implications of Nuclear War, 1986, p 16 & 64.

41. Fire and the related effects of nuclear explosions, Proceedings of the 1982 Asilomar Conference, p VI-28

42. Problems of fire in nuclear warfare, JE Hill, RAND, 21 August 1961.

43. Defending against allied bombing campaign: air raid shelters and gas protection in Germany 1939-1945, S Cromwell, Institute for historical review,

44. Possible fatalities from superfires, T Postol, Medical Implications of Nuclear War, 1986, p 64.

45. Interactions and spreading of adjacent large area fires, Defense Nuclear Agency, March 1986,

46. Vulnerability of populations and the urban health care systems to nuclear weapon attack – examples for four American cities. WC Bell & CE Dallas, 2007, p 5.

47. Analyzine Evacuation Versus Shelter-in-Place Strategies After a Terrorist Nuclear Detonation, LM Wein, Y Choi & S Denuit, Risk Analysis.

Sword of Damocles

*Trish Whitham,
Janet Fenton,
Rob Edwards,
Tim Streeet,
Peter Burt,
Alan Charlton*

In November 2022, there was a webinar hosted by the Nuclear Information Service to commemorate John Ainslie's work and to launch his archive. This is a partial transcript.

Trish Whitham: I am the coordinator of the Nuclear Information Service and also the project manager for the Ainslie Archive, a work in progress that's available online. The archive project was enabled by donations from a great many individuals as well as some grants, covering the costs of scanning, categorising and uploading John's vast archive. It has also covered the cost of the website work we've had to do, with about a thousand documents available and many, many more to come. There are some interesting stories coming, after which the event will be opened up for discussion and further contributions.

Our first speaker is Janet Fenton. Janet worked closely with John Ainslie for many years. She's currently secretary of the Scottish Parliament Disarmament Cross Party Group, organiser of the Secure Scotland Core Group and Vice Chair of Scottish CND. She's worked with Acronym Institute, Peace and Justice Scotland and the International Campaign to Abolish Nuclear Weapons. Janet is a co-founder of Secure Scotland and a member of Trident Ploughshares.

Janet Fenton: It was my pleasure and an honour to work with John Ainslie. I've been thinking and thinking and I can't actually remember when I first met him. I think that's partly because he was such a modest and unassuming person. I might well have met him when he was staffing a stall somewhere or envelope stuffing in the office. But certainly on the initial meeting, you would never imagine that you were bumping into somebody who was such a powerhouse in terms of his capacity as a researcher. And you certainly wouldn't think that you were meeting a minister of the Church of Scotland or an arrested activist, somebody who had jumped in a canoe to buzz Trident submarines coming up the Clyde. John was a man of enormous passion for our work on disarmament. He seemed to be able to slip from one identity to another very readily.

I remember on one occasion having to call at his home to either give him something or collect something. He was in the kitchen, standing at the ironing board with a bunch of t-shirts for teddies, ironing CND symbols onto the front. Obviously on that day this seemed like an important task to John. But you could also meet him running after Brian Coyle, making sure that he got the photographs of nuclear convoy activity.

At one point my daughter, Mary, was resident at the Faslane Peace Camp around the time of the International Court of Justice ruling on nuclear weapons. People were putting their arms in concrete 'lock-ons' – a bit of a rarity then, but more familiar now. My daughter was doing that and she somewhat nervously 'locked-on' at the South Gate of the base. The police were not really aware of 'lock-ons' at the time and started to move her in a slightly dangerous fashion. She remembered that somebody had said to shout for cameras if that happened and she shouted for cameras. Mary looked above her head and there was John Ainslie, up a tree, taking photographs of her.

John's work as the administrator of Scottish CND was incomparable, really, partly because he was very idiosyncratic in the way that he did the job. When I spoke about him chasing convoys or chasing Brian Coyle chasing convoys, the thing with John was that he was not only the kind of activist who would perform imaginatively and quickly in that situation to take direct action. At the same time, he would also have a really careful note of every single vehicle that was in the convoy, what it meant and and what it was likely to be carrying.

His research on the UK's nuclear weapons system was a hugely important part of the international disarmament campaign, which he followed very closely. It was very common that you would walk into the office at lunchtime and John would be eating his sandwiches and at the same time he'd be watching either the parliamentary process or what was happening at the United Nations on the internet. He was able to provide hugely effective and useful briefings for people who were travelling to those kinds of meeting and doing their best to take the campaign forward in that particular way. His briefings could be about simple campaigning activity for new volunteers, or they could be at a very high level of technical expertise, or from a very politically astute understanding of the ramifications of what was happening at the UN and around the world.

I remember asking when he decided to stop being a church minister and start being involved with all this anti-nuclear weapons activity. He looked at me rather strangely and said that "once you're a minister of the Church of Scotland, if you've been ordained as a minister of the Church of Scotland, that's it." I realised that he felt there was not any confusion between those two roles.

I had the privilege of spending a week with John in a residential learning situation in northern France. We also spent a week doing the Rowntree Peace Leadership Programme and that was another opportunity to really get to know John in a different kind of way and for all of us to understand and learn together.

He was very keen always to express the very particular Scottish input to nuclear disarmament in a global way and really understood the very unique position Scotland is in with regard to that. He was very strongly behind Scotland's peace initiative and he had his own style of dividing these different areas of work. John always maintained that the research work that he did was quite separate from his role as coordinator of Scottish CND.

I'm looking forward to hearing from Rob Edwards because I really don't understand how somebody became so expert in getting information from people using Freedom of Information rules, sending questions to America and Canada before that was a possibility in the UK. I also feel that it's very important to make clear how important the nuclear issue was to John for very, very basic reasons. He was such a strong family man. His love for his family and the attention that he paid to his family, his sharing the joy and pleasure of his adventures and work with his son, Duncan, with those of us who were around him, was very significant. John was devastated by the loss of Duncan, but didn't change his approach to the work in any way.

In one of his last interviews, John talked about children's hospitals in Moscow and spoke very movingly about the possible impact of the UK's nuclear weapons policy on those hospitals. The humanitarian impact of nuclear weapons was always at the heart of John's view of these things.

Trish Witham: Thanks very much for sharing that with us. What a multi-talented person. So now we're going to move on to Rob Edwards. Rob has been a freelance environmental journalist and nuclear muckraker for more than 40 years. He's written for the *New Scientist*, *The Guardian*, *Scotland on Sunday*, *Sunday Herald* and many others. He's now a journalist with *The Ferret*, an award winning platform for investigative journalism in Scotland. He also worked very closely with John Ainslie over many years.

Rob Edwards: Thank you very much. And thank you, Janet, for your words about John, all of which I would endorse. I knew and worked with John for a long time, many decades. It's an honour, a privilege, to be here to pay tribute to him and his work and to tell a few stories about him, which is essentially what I'm going to do.

I've been a journalist for more than 40 years now and for a lot of that time in all the bowels of freelance writing about nuclear matters. It was a particular interest of mine, as it was of John's.

The first thing I want to say is, as a journalist, without your sources, you're nothing. Without your contacts, without the people you speak to or the people who speak to you, then there's nothing to write. There's nothing to know, there are no stories to be done because without sources, without contacts, you can't do your job.

So the trouble is that the longer you go on, the more valuable sources become ill and die. When John died in 2016, he deprived the movement of one of its most effective operators. When he died, the tributes came from all over the place, from CND and others in the peace movement. But there were also tributes from Nicola Sturgeon, Jeremy Corbyn (leader of the Labour Party at the time), the Scottish Greens and many others. They all said very nice things about John after he died.

His death also left me without the best source of stories I've ever had on nuclear weapons. I tried to figure out this morning how many times I've quoted John in stories, but I didn't have time to count them all. There are hundreds, literally hundreds of stories over the years in which he played a role. I'm just going to refer to a few highlights to give an indication of the kind of things he was doing.

For example, in 2013, there was a story in *The Guardian* that was entirely founded on a report that John had written, which basically argued that Trident submarines could not be shifted from Faslane on the Clyde to Devonport on the south coast of England. John had discovered that Devonport didn't have the correct safety clearances and would be unlikely to get them. So of course that story is very important in the whole debate about the role of Trident post-Scottish independence, which is why he wrote the report.

John was always ahead of the game, immediately realising that it was a possibility that if Scotland voted for independence, Trident would have to be moved. He immediately started assessing the possibility of where it could move to and became really expert on the options and how none of them quite worked out from all sorts of points of view.

Another story from 2011 was done with *The Guardian* and Channel Four News. John had done a Freedom of Information request – which he was an expert at – to the Ministry of Defence, and this unearthed a very heavily censored report revealing in essence that the reactors that run on nuclear submarines were potentially vulnerable to a fatal nuclear accident and failed to meet modern safety standards. That was a report known at the time as the MacFarlane report, which was written by a senior submarine person in the MoD and really exposed for the first time and in much detail, the kind of dangers that we were risking by running these old, clapped out, not very well designed submarine reactors.

The footnote to that is that after we did the story, John came to me and said he'd realised that his version of this MacFarlane report had been very poorly redacted. Large sections of text that were blacked out, but if you simply cut and pasted them into a Word document or another document, you could reveal all the hidden text. That's a kind of schoolboy information error that's been made several times by the Ministry of Defence and other government departments, where they don't do the redaction properly. This caused something of a palaver at the time. Along with others, John decided to publish the full version of the report, showing in more detail how UK nuclear submarines were unsafe and the sailors who worked in them were more at risk of having an accident and dying at sea. That was a big story at the time and it wouldn't have been possible without John.

Another important story was in *New Scientist* in 2008. John had been doing an awful lot of research in the US archives, where there was more freedom of information on nuclear issues than there ever has been in the UK. Here he discovered that the US was experiencing problems with a mysterious but vital component of the Trident warhead known as Fog Bank. It's never really been nailed down as far as I'm aware. Fog Bank is suspected of being a highly flammable and explosive foam in the warheads. Because of the research he'd done, we were able to reveal that the US and the UK were having a problem with its Fog Bank when they were trying to extend its life in 2006.

Here's a story from *The Sunday Herald*. John got hold of a leaked Ministry of Defence 'wargaming' scenario. So there was to be a big military exercise in Scotland. It was quite funny, if in a sort of dark way, because the Ministry of Defence renamed Scotland 'Brown Air' for the purposes of the scenario. At the time they said that was nothing to do with the fact that Gordon Brown was about to become Prime Minister. It was just the colour they chose. The scenario also invented a sinister terrorist group in the Inner Hebrides. I can remember John laughing as he was explaining all this to me on the phone.

Another story from 2010. I was involved in challenging the Ministry of

Defence to release the Annual Nuclear Safety Report. John was one of those who helped me. He did a great deal of work along with others for no money whatsoever, so that we could challenge the decision of the military not to release these Annual Nuclear Safety Reports. Rather unexpectedly, we won at the last minute when they backed down, resulting in the annual safety reports being revealed. This gave us an unprecedented insight into the problems they thought they were facing, mainly to do with staff shortages and skill shortages. But then in 2017, the committee retrenched, made three reports secret, and it all went dark again. The rules for Freedom of Information were taken up by Peter Burt, who has since challenged the Committee on Secrecy, so far unsuccessfully.

Another story that John was involved with, which was very big at the time, was another *Guardian* and Channel Four thing in 2009. He was, along with others and me, involved in doing a co-ordinated Freedom of Information request to various organisations in Scotland to try and find out more about environmental problems at Fastlane. This ended up revealing that according to documents the Scottish Protection Agency released at the time, there had been a series of previously unreported leaks of radioactive coolant from submarine reactors into the Clyde in 2004, 2007, 2008. We have been less successful since then at finding out such things.

This is the last story. It is one of the biggest stories I've ever been involved with and probably one of the most important. It wouldn't have happened without John and it was a front page splash in the *The Sunday Herald* in 2015. The introduction to the story said Trident submarines are plagued by serious safety lapses, beset by multiple blunders, and are a disaster waiting to happen, according to a nuclear weapons engineer turned whistleblower, now hunted by the police. The whistleblower was, of course, William McNeilly, a Royal Navy man on HMS *Victorious*, who was subsequently arrested and then dishonourably discharged by the Navy.

The week before that story broke was probably one of the most memorable in my journalistic career. As I said, none of it would have happened without John. I was remembering why this morning. The reason why is that he read his emails. I mean, he didn't just read his emails. He *really* read his emails, which I suspect not all of us do. John and many others, including me, had been sent emails by William McNeilly, linking to a long report he'd written about his time on HMS *Victorious* and about the problems that he had witnessed and had been part of. But it was John who read it first, grasped its significance and called me and highlighted it and started the ball rolling. I, of course, then had to go to the Ministry of Defence to see whether this was true, whether he existed and what had happened. And for days, the MOD failed to get back to me. I can remember late on a Friday night not knowing whether we had a story for that Sunday's paper or not. And then at the very last minute, the MOD got back to me, confirmed that McNeilly had been a member of the Royal Navy and had absconded and they were looking for him and, in essence, confirming a story. Then we were able to run the front page splash about it. None of that would have happened if it hadn't been for John's diligence. That's how I remember him. He was diligent in the extreme and he really cared for facts and honesty, which I think admirable traits.

Final thought? A personal note. I mean, aside from his diligence, the thing I most admired about John was his diffidence. Janet mentioned this. A lot of those people who seek out journalists are the opposite of diffident, they want to be quoted. They want to have their names in the papers. They want, in some way or another, to promote themselves. I have dealt with many people who would fall into that category. But that was never the case with John. He was self-effacing, absolutely shy. He never sought the limelight.

Trish Whitham: We now have Tim Street. Tim is a board member at Nuclear Information Service, and he's also Secretary of British Pugwash. He's been working on peace and disarmament issues since 2005 and has been very closely involved in the digitising and publishing of John Ainslie's Research Archive. He has also worked with Campaign Against the Arms Trade, the International Campaign to Abolish Nuclear Weapons, the British-American Security Information Council, Oxford Research Group, Conscience, the Campaign to Stop Killer Robots and Drone Wars UK.

Tim Street: I was lucky to meet John in 2010 in Scotland when I started working for ICAN. I went up to Scotland to a talk at the Scottish Trades Union Congress. I took away a lot from that meeting. John picked me up from the station and as has been said, he was very diffident, a shy, unassuming, just a very nice, warm person. You quickly realise that you're dealing with someone with hidden depths, shall we say. John was very warm and lovely and kind and thoughtful, but also a great researcher. He asked the right questions. I feel like I've got a bit of a grasp on nuclear issues having worked on it for a few years. But then you go back to John's publications and you think, "Wow", because he had a really different level of understanding of the technical issues, which takes hours and hours of persistent study and dogged determination to develop. John was impressive both as a person and as a researcher.

I'm very honoured to be working on John's archive. For the last year or so, working with the members of the NIS team, we have been digitising the archive. We are about three quarters of the way through that and have uploaded thousands of his documents to the website. His archive contains documents relating to nuclear weapons that were collected over several decades. The information comes from a wide range of sources, including official US and UK government files, as well as some Russian documents. There's also activist correspondence, civil society reports, photos, graphs, newsletters and media articles. Working on the archive is very interesting for the insights it provides on how John approached the issues, how he found his way in and what his focus was, the way he thought about them, what he found interesting.

His archive covers things like the UK-US special nuclear relationship and the Mutual Defence Agreement, as well as preparations in the UK in the 1980s for civil defence in the event of a nuclear attack. These questions are being raised again today.

The archive includes original documents from the fifties and sixties, so John also had an historical interest in issues in the National Archives, such as the nitty-gritty of how British strategy on nuclear planning came to be. That includes the Moscow criterion and how many nuclear weapons would be needed to obliterate Moscow and its leadership. It also includes the geography and importance of the many nuclear weapons installations in the UK, mapping what nuclear facilities and associated installations and technical facilities are in the UK, which is again a very hidden or often invisible aspect of the US-UK nuclear special relationship. We've taken measures to make the archive website as accessible as possible. We're going to keep on trying to tell the story that John put together in the most accessible way of all.

I wanted to talk really briefly about what the 'Sword of Damocles' means. Then I'll talk about what we can do. John's website was called 'The Sword of Damocles', and it was the home to many of his publications which we are trying to get back online. In the ancient parable, The Sword of Damocles refers to the predicament of the very powerful, surrounded by enemies. Their lives are full of anxiety and paranoia, and they labour under the constant fear of attack and death. At the onset of the nuclear age, the Sword of Damocles came to refer to the existential dangers looming over us all. And there is a particularly strange and cruel twist to the parable, because the people of the world don't have the power of kings or their riches. Yet we are condemned to live with the daily threat of extinction. The very powerful rule the world through nuclear terror, which they like to call 'national security', and the 'global rules based order' that risks destroying everything. This must lead people to ask, 'how can we extricate ourselves from this situation?' This is a question John's work directly seeks to answer and contributes to answering.

In October 2022, US President Joe Biden commented that the risk of Armageddon is at its highest level since the Cuban Missile Crisis. During that crisis probability of nuclear war might have been as high as 50%. US Defence Secretary, Robert McNamara, recognised that it was only luck that prevented nuclear war. In 1962 the US would not tolerate Soviet missiles in Cuba providing a 'deterrent' against invasion. Today, Russia won't tolerate NATO expanding to its borders and stationing offensive missiles with very short flight times to Moscow. The big picture is that the longer the Ukraine conflict, following Putin's illegal invasion, drags on the greater the possibility of miscalculation involving Russia. This risks escalation, with a huge deployment of conventional weapons and the risk of nuclear use at a time when national resources should be focused on the climate crisis.

The Ukraine conflict has also led to soaring military spending. Liz Truss committed to an extra £157 billion in defence spending, which, if the UK Government goes ahead with that pledge, would mean an annual defence budget of £100 billion in 2030. In terms of Trident, the estimated total costs of replacing it between 2019 and 2027 are at least £172 billion. Meanwhile, the US is set to spend more than $1 trillion over the next 30 years on developing a new range of nuclear weapons. So we are clearly in a very dangerous, unstable, militarising situation. We really need to be heading in the opposite direction.

We need many, many people to be dedicated and to have the tools and the courage and curiosity that people like John had. John's example was to focus on democracy, transparency and accountability. He made nuclear weapons visible and intelligible. He provided clear and coherent proposals in direct, clear language on how to get rid of Trident.

I want to end by thinking how we get rid of Trident? How can we think and what we can do? The way I look at it is to try and think through – to mentally construct – and link how the conflict in Ukraine could end, how that would impact what happens in the UK, how we eventually get a nuclear-weapons-free world, and think what could I do to help contribute even a little bit to making that a little bit more possible. If you get to start thinking about that or find it difficult, then check out John's work and he'll provide you with inspiration and ideas on what to do.

Trish Whitham: Thanks a lot, Tim. It's nice to end on a hopeful note of what we can do. Peter Burt is our next speaker. Peter was the programme director of the Nuclear Information Service for a number of years.
Peter Burt: Thank you so much for arranging this session today. How

lovely it's been to hear all the stories of John and bring back all the memories. I think this is a really special occasion and I'm very grateful to you for your work in arranging this.

I was working quite closely with John about ten years ago when I was with NIS. We spoke maybe two or three times a week on the phone. I was fortunate to meet John for the first time at the Joseph Rowntree Peace Leadership event that Janet mentioned at the beginning of the session. And of course, that was the first time that I met Janet as well. And that set up quite a nice little alliance between us all to go forward and do some quite exciting work together in the weeks and months and years after that.

People have mentioned the Freedom of Information research that John did over the years. I'd like to draw attention to some of the other stuff that John did as well, because, as you may know, John had many other remarkable things he'd done in his life. It all started in the military, and I believe he was in the signals side of things and had some knowledge and some background in intelligence. I think he probably used all his intelligence skills in the research work he did.

So, for example, he was always willing – as well as sitting behind a desk and studying – to get out there and put his boots on the ground, get out there in the field to get real life evidence. If you look on the Scottish CND websites, you can find video footage that he took of HMS Vanguard limping into Faslane after the collision that it had in 2009 with a French submarine in the Bay of Biscay. On many occasions, he went out to spot the nuclear convoys and film them. He also had many, many sources as well. I'd like to remind you of some of the early work that John did, which people haven't perhaps spoken about so much yet.

Back in the early 1990s, the UK submarine fleet was undergoing real problems when cracks developed in the reactors in crucial parts of the pipework. John was able to reveal that and blow the whistle due to his sources, his whistleblowers inside the Faslane base. If you look at the archive, then you'll find a report, *Cracking Under the Pressure*, that tells the story and gives some of the information that the whistleblowers passed on to John.

John put together *The Future of the British Bomb* in 2006 with the WMD Awareness Project. I think that to this day, that is still one of the definitive papers explaining how Britain's bomb works and how the Trident programme works. If you look at the footnotes to that paper, then you'll get an idea of the absolutely meticulous and painstaking way that John went about doing his research. You'll see that he travels through hundreds and hundreds of contacts in the United States to get all the details about flight control software and missile procurement. And he also went through dozens and dozens of online job adverts of the Atomic Weapons Establishment to get an idea of what the scientists there were working on and what the status of the programme was.

So he really did use all his skills to put together various research notes and research papers. I think another paper which he put together, which hasn't been mentioned so much – but which in my opinion was absolutely the most important piece of work that he ever did – was a paper called *Dismantling Trident*. He put this together to show how the UK Trident missiles could be dismantled in the event of a decision by the government to disarm. He showed that it was really a very simple matter that could take place literally over a period of months, if not less, to disarm the warheads taken off submarines and start decommissioning again at the Atomic Weapons Establishment. That was a hugely valuable piece of work.

I think it's important to recognise the work that John did after Scottish CND decided that it was going to support the Yes Scotland campaign about ten years or so ago. John played an important part in pushing nuclear disarmament and the demand that Trident should leave Scotland to the centre of the Yes Scotland campaign.

I'm sure if John was sitting here listening to us go on, he would be cringing and would be very, very embarrassed about the kind and fulsome tributes that we're paying to him. Because as we've heard, he was very modest and very self-effacing. But I think it's impossible to underestimate the commitment that he gave to nuclear disarmament in this country during his much appreciated life.

Trish Whitham: Thank you, Peter. That was really interesting. I didn't know about the intelligence aspect and that helps to explain the meticulousness of his research. Alan Charlton is our next contributor.

Alan Charlton: I'd like to endorse everything that's been said about John. When I think of John, the memory that comes back to me immediately is of the time when a group of us were out on the little boat that we used to hire to go up the Firth of Clyde to do some protesting. John was in his inflatable beside the boat being followed very closely by three MoD inflatables, navy high powered ones. There were obviously MoD personnel on it. It was quite intimidating, actually, because they're all in these wet suits with balaclavas and they're holding the long range camera lenses over their shoulders. They were chasing John and John manoeuvred in and out of the way. But eventually they managed to corner him, took the inflatable over, and John got dunked in the water. He was arrested and charged, and a few weeks later he was in front of a Sheriff in Dumbarton.

And what the MoD didn't understand was that the Sheriff, I'm not sure if he was a member of CND or was sympathetic, dismissed the charges against John and suggested that the Admiralty should be charged with endangering life. John found that quite amusing. He was just such a humble man and he embodied the virtues that I think are so important: courage with compassion and capability. His sense of humour was wonderful as was his sense of adventure. I believe that one of the last things he said when he was preparing for his own death was that he was just embarking on the next big adventure. And that said it all about John. I'll never forget him. Thank you.

* * *

Webinar
The Sword of Damocles
Reflections on the life and work of nuclear researcher and activist John Ainslie

With Janet Fenton, Scottish CND; Tom Unterrainer, Bertrand Russell Peace Foundation; Rob Edwards, investigative journalist; and Dr Tim Street, NIS.

14:00 GMT, 9 November 2022

Register
www.nuclearinfo.org

NIS Nuclear Information Service

A full recording of the webinar is available on the Nuclear Information Servive YouTube channel:
www.youtube.com/watch?v=Npm1q0VMTvs

Gerald Holtom

Designer of the Peace Symbol

Gerald Holtom
Designer of the Peace Symbol

Darius Holtom

The Peace Symbol is instantly recognised the world over. It continues to appear as wars and nuclear threats darken our prospects, decade after decade. Where does it come from and what does it mean?

In this affectionate biography, Darius Holtom recounts how his father, Gerald, developed the design that became the Peace Symbol. Gerald Holtom changed our world through his creativity, compassion and skill.

"The Peace Symbol is familiar to millions: the movement for nuclear disarmament needs Gerald's example to become familiar once more."
Tom Unterrainer
Chair of the Campaign for Nuclear Disarmament

ISBN 9780851249155 | £7.99

www.spokesmanbooks.org

▲ At dinner: Edith Russell, Bertrand Russell, Ralph Schoenman, Pattle Pottle, Christopher Farley, Alastair Yule, Susan Potter

Christopher Farley
1934-2022

'Without his judgement and thoughtfulness we should be hard put to it to keep on as even a keel as we manage to keep. But he is reticent and unassuming and too often remains in the background. He takes a point quickly, and I thought at first that his occasional hesitation in pronouncing upon it was owing to timidity. I now know that it is owing to extreme scrupulousness. It was some time before I realised the depth of feeling with which he pursues justice or the compassion and patience with which this pursuit is tempered. I learned only gradually that his obvious knowledge of present-day men and affairs is enriched by wide reading and a very considerable study of the past. The tendency to dogmatism and claptrap and humbug which this combination might induce in a more superficial mind is burnt away by his intense perception of ironies and absurdity and the liveliness of his many interests. His observations are both sensitive and his own. All this makes him a helpful, interesting and delightful companion.'

Bertrand Russell's considered endorsement of Christopher Farley first appeared in 1969 in Volume Three of Russell's *Autobiography*. By that time, Farley had been working closely with Russell for several years, going back to the early 1960s and the Committee of 100 in Britain, which pledged itself to civil disobedience and non-violent direct action against British nuclear weapons and testing. So Russell had plenty of personal experience on which to base his generous appreciation of Farley, who returned the compliment and supported the Russells with great care, attention and energy.

In November 1964, Russell entrusted to Farley the delicate mission to Vietnam as his representative at the International Conference for Solidarity with the Vietnamese People against American Imperialism — For the Defence of Peace, which was held in Hanoi. By this time, the Bertrand Russell Peace Foundation had been established and Farley was centrally involved in all its public campaigns as well as its internal organisation. In 1967, the International War Crimes Tribunal heard eyewitness testimony of the atrocities being committed in Vietnam by US forces. Less flamboyant than Ralph Schoenman, Russell's American secretary, Farley helped keep the show on the road through these turbulent, exciting and expensive campaigns and events of Russell's last years during the 1960s.

While the Vietnam Tribunal was doing its work, Farley led a separate delegation to the Middle East to see first-hand the situation of the Palestinian refugees following the Arab-Israeli Six-Day War in June 1967. Chris seemed to be constantly on the move. In Cairo in 1970, he delivered Bertrand Russell's final public message, composed two days before his death on 2 February, which continues to resonate:

> '... *The tragedy of the people of Palestine is that their country was "given" by a foreign Power to another people for the creation of a new State. The result was that many hundreds of thousands of innocent people were made permanently homeless ...*'

In addition to his extensive travels on behalf of the Foundation, Chris served as its Secretary during the early years from its establishment in January 1964. He composed and filed extensive correspondence, frequently travelling between London and North Wales, where the Russells lived. Sometimes he travelled via Nottingham, where his trumpet echoed around the Foundation's offices as he practised jazz favourites. Chris earned the trust of Bertrand and Edith Russell and, when Lord Russell died in 1970, Chris was an executor of his will. Edith died on 1 January 1978, and Chris was her executor alongside Ken Coates. Chris also served as one of Bertrand Russell's literary executors.

In 1971, Chris and Ken Coates journeyed to Beijing where they met with Chinese Premier Zhou Enlai as well as Prince Norodom Sihanouk of Cambodia, who was living in China in exile from the conflict which US President Nixon had extended to his country from Vietnam.

During the eight years that Edith survived Bertrand Russell, Chris frequently made the long journey to Plas Penrhyn, the Russells' leased house near Porthmadog. Edith evidently appreciated his company and support. After she died, he packed up the house, including her papers, which she had already carefully sorted with his assistance. The Edith Russell Collection now forms part of the Bertrand Russell Archives at McMaster University, Canada, where it is being catalogued.

Tony Simpson

Beijing 1971: Christopher Farley and Ken Coates meet Premier Zhou Enlai

Chris Farley
An Appreciation

During the two years when I worked with Bertrand Russell and his Foundation, 1966 to 1968, Chris Farley was the steadiest and most thoughtful member of the team that steered the Foundation through that turbulent time. I met him by correspondence some months earlier and worked with him subsequently, when I had a generous grant from the related charity, the Atlantic Peace Foundation, to conduct research on chemical and bacteriological weapons. Sadly, we lost touch after I returned to the United States permanently in 1970. None the less, he remained with me as a moral compass, and even after half a century I miss him as a friend and colleague remembered for his wit and wisdom.

Before I joined the Foundation in London, I had corresponded with Lord Russell and the three members of his Foundation who were central to its work during my own tenure, Chris, Ralph Schoenman, and Pamela Wood. In 1964, the Foundation decided to publish an essay that I had written on the Vietnam War in a pamphlet that was also to include Lord Russell's essay, *War and Atrocity in Vietnam*. It sold for two shillings and six pence. Chris worked tirelessly and invisibly behind the scenes as editor, fact-checker, and stylist, eliminating any duplicative material and giving the pamphlet its coherence. Decades before there were faxes and e-mail, we worked together long distance with air letters.

Chris was always the practical member of the Foundation's board of directors who kept it afloat in the early years before its finances were more stable. When I arrived in London to join the Foundation's team at Shavers Place, he introduced himself in person – and then asked if the Foundation could borrow whatever funds I had at the time of my travel to ensure that it could avoid an overdraft when writing payroll cheques. (In due course, this small but unexpected loan was repaid.) The Foundation had embarked on a plan to hold an international war crimes tribunal at Lord Russell's invitation. Chris was the realist who knew that we needed a budget, as well as ambitious fund raising. He saw that the bills were paid and oversaw the dramatic staff expansion that the tribunal required. Chris also directed the Foundation's publishing capacity as occasional papers, pamphlets, and newsletters gave way to the launch of *The Spokesman*.

I worked for several months in Plas Penrhyn in 1967 after Lord Russell stopped travelling to London, and Chris Farley was the point person who kept us apprised of developments at our Shavers Place offices in

Piccadilly. Similarly, when the war crimes tribunal was under way, first in Stockholm and later in Roskilde (outside Copenhagen), it was Chris who moved into Plas Penrhyn to convey information back and forth between Lord Russell and the tribunal, including Russell's own comments on crucial issues.

I should have said at the outset that two of Chris's distinguishing qualities were his selflessness and energy – not manic energy, but indefatigable stamina when the work just required more hours in the day and more days in the calendar. He put in all this time with no expectation of seeing his own name celebrated for things that could not have been accomplished without him. I was about a decade younger than Chris and Ralph, but it was always a challenge to keep up with them.

Both Bertrand and Edith Russell trusted and respected Chris, and I think their activism had evolved together from the nuclear disarmament campaigns of the earlier1960s to the focus on Vietnam and other human rights issues in the later period. They were all deeply worried about the risk of nuclear war, the environmental consequences of nuclear testing, and the plight of political dissidents throughout the world. And everyone appreciated Chris's ability to put a smile on our faces in the darkest times. He had a superb ability to skewer pompous politicians and to expose what Lord Russell appropriately referred to as claptrap and humbug.

We are all creatures of our own time. Chris endured the German bombings in his childhood and the need to move to safer areas of the countryside. He came of age as the US and Soviet superpowers put the human race at risk. As Lord Russell's emissary, he made an early journey to Vietnam and observed the horror of that war before most of the Western media had appreciated the war's human cost.

It is fitting that *The Spokesman* honour the memory of one of its founders, a gentle but firm voice for liberty and social justice in a century that repeatedly put both at risk. We can best respect his memory by continuing that work.

Russell Stetler

Reviews

Africa

John Pampallis and Maryke Bailey, *A Brief History of South Africa: From the Earliest Times to the Mandela Presidency,* Jacana Media, 2021, 360 pages, paperback ISBN 9781928232957, £12.99

I used to say the year 1652 must be inscribed on my forehead. That was the date drilled into young South African minds in the 1950s to mark 'the beginning of our country's history'. The erasure of anything beyond a white European colonial narrative was the norm under apartheid as it was in Britain. Even in the mid 1960s, Hugh Trevor-Roper, Oxford's Regius Professor of Modern History, could declare: 'There is only the history of Europe in Africa. The rest is largely darkness ... and darkness is not a subject for history.'

It took the work of historians such as Belgian Jan Vansina, Nigeria's Kenneth Dike and Jacob Ajayi, and British scholars Roland Oliver and John Fage to address this ignorance of Africa. But, perhaps more than any other writer, it was British historian-cum-journalist (and ex-WW2 Partisan) Basil Davidson who for over fifty years actively disseminated knowledge about the continent's past and present – including colonial shadows, ongoing challenges of development, and key questions of capitalism or socialism.

John Pampallis has been involved in education throughout his working life, including nine years teaching at the African National Congress's school for young exiles in Tanzania. From 1989, he was involved in ANC education policy development as well as publishing a number of books on South African history. Maryke Bailey, co-author of *A Brief History of South Africa*, is a history teacher. The book is essentially, but not exclusively, a resource for teachers or study groups, formal or informal. The suggested educational activities aim to encourage critical thinking and debate among students.

Part A consists of a chronological narrative from pre-17th century societies to the Mandela Presidency (1994-1999). The second part revolves around nine themes: Economy; Bantustans; Schooling; Poverty and Inequality; Life under Apartheid – Urban and Rural; Women's Struggles; Trade Union Movement; South Africa's Constitutions; International Solidarity Against Apartheid.

Each chapter in both sections is followed by Discussion Questions in which the authors encourage readers to explore and probe historical legacies, as well as to debate 'What's to be done?' These are followed by lists of Additional Readings. Many of these refer to online resources, including documents digitalized for South African History Online. Finally, an Appendix for Teachers consists of 60 pages of Text Engagement Activities (which can be photocopied), followed by an Index.

Inevitably, the huge task of condensing the complex narratives of South Africa into 'A Brief History' leads to omissions. With Themes considered from a contemporary perspective, I would have liked to see Corruption as a separate theme. It is mentioned, in passing, under the theme of South Africa's Bantustans where the authors note 'many bantustans developed into one-party states that were supported by the apartheid security forces'. (p206) However, there's much more to understand about the roots of contemporary corruption. Prof Steven Friedman dates it back to Jan van Riebeeck and colonization in 1652. ('How corruption in South Africa is deeply rooted in the country's past and why that matters', 28.8.2020)

I would also have appreciated a theme focused on the Culture of Violence, pulling together violations of human rights by the apartheid government and, as acknowledged at the Truth and Reconciliation Commission, 'killings and torture in MK [uMkhonto we Sizwe] camps, committed by itself [ANC] and its allies during the course of the struggle'. (p184) I would have liked the authors to explore the differences in culture of the ANC as an exiled political organization engaged in military struggle and the culture of emerging trade unions and civil rights organizations inside the country, pushing for militant but non-violent negotiation.

Despite its gaps, *A Brief History of South Africa* is a commendable resource for teachers and students. The authors are realistic about how much remains unfulfilled in terms of constitutional rights. For example, under the theme of Women's Struggles, after citing some of the victories, they conclude that 'Patriarchal attitudes persist at all levels of society… the triple oppression of race, class and gender, although officially illegal, remains a fact of life for most of them. Eliminating it remains one of the big challenges of a democratic South Africa'. (p259) I think readers will come away from this book conscious not just of the struggle so far but of how many challenges South Africans still face ahead.

Beverley Naidoo

Childhood under occupation

Beverley Naidoo, *Children of the Stone City*, HarperCollins Children's Books, 2022, 272 pages, hardback ISBN 9780008471743, £12.99

Beverley Naidoo grew up in a South Africa which was bitterly divided by apartheid. As a student in the early 1960s she began to question the privileges that she enjoyed and became active in the anti-apartheid movement, eventually moving to Britain in the late 1960s. From the effects of apartheid to the trauma of refugees and asylum seekers, her books explore the experiences of children living under pressure.

Now in her eighties, Naidoo is as perceptive as ever, tackling issues of inequality, the arbitrary abuse of power, and the role of advocacy. In her latest Young Adult novel, *Children of the Stone City*, we are again given the perspective of children caught up in a bewildering system of oppression which has divided society into the powerful 'Permitteds' and the powerless 'Nons'. We are not told where in the world the Stone City is, nor are we told what distinguishes the Permitteds from the Nons. Apart from a later reference to language, there seem to be no obvious differences such as skin colour or religion.

We can see features of the society which are familiar from both historical and current examples. In the first chapter we are told that the children 'avoided using the alleys where Permitted flags hung out of windows in houses that not long ago had belonged to Non families'. Later, we see an eviction with household goods piled up on the street while a Permitted family takes possession of a former Non home. Nons require a permit to live and work in the Stone City; the Permitted Police is a fearsome presence and failure to obtain a permit means banishment beyond The Wall.

It's several years since I worked in schools and I wondered what connections a young reader might make, so asked Martha, aged 14, to read the book and report back. Martha recognised elements of apartheid, having read one of Naidoo's earlier books, but also the Berlin Wall and, more recently, Trump's Border Wall. She also agreed with me that the ambiguity of the setting was deliberate and gave the story a sense of universality to challenge our notions of power and discrimination anywhere in the world.

Naidoo gives her readers an insight into the consequences of a divisive system through the lives of three children, Adam aged 12, his younger sister Leila, and their friend Zak. In the early chapters we see the importance of family and community support, especially when Adam and Leila's father dies suddenly, leaving the renewal of their mother's permit looking precarious. If she loses the permit the family will have to leave the city, putting an end to the children's attendance at music school. For Adam, a talented violinist, this would be the end of all his dreams.

Adam's grandmother explains that these divisions were not always the case. In the 'Time Before' the two groups lived amicably side by side and were all governed by the 'OverPower'. Then terrible things happened to the Permitteds 'OverSeas' and many 'came here'. It was when some Permitted leaders claimed that the land belonged to them and nobody else that the trouble started.

By now an adult reader can recognise the conflicting claims of Israelis and Palestinians. This is a topic which receives little attention in schools, largely because it is so politically sensitive, and teachers are wary of the fine line between criticism of the State of Israel and anti-Semitism.

In her Author's Note at the end of the book, Naidoo explains that she was inspired to write this story after meeting young Palestinian readers but that she left her setting deliberately ambiguous. 'I hope readers may be stirred to think about the consequences for all children in societies powerfully divided into Permitteds and Nons.' She points out that Permitteds and Nons can exist anywhere. Indeed, in her own case she was born in South Africa as a Permitted, but had she been born in Occupied Europe in 1943 to her Jewish mother, she would have been a Non.

In *Children of the Stone City* we are drawn into this frightening world. Adam has been well schooled by his father to avoid trouble and keep clear of potential confrontation with Permitteds. Zak is more headstrong and a brush with a group of Permitted youths leads to a midnight police raid on the homes of both boys and their arrest as terrorists. Despite their youth, Adam and Zak are subjected to 'questioning' by the police, which is designed to break them physically and intimidate them into signing false confessions written in a language they can't read. Adam understands what is happening and resists just long enough for help to arrive in the shape of a campaigning Permitted lawyer, Ms Roth. Zak on the other hand, alone, frightened and physically abused, signs a confession and is trapped within the system. Adam now faces the increased danger of his mother's permit being revoked. His only hope is to use his musical talent to attract the attention of a visiting famous violinist who might speak up on their behalf and expose to the world the injustices within the Stone City.

I found the treatment of the boys in police custody shocking, as did Martha, but she was aware that such things could and do happen to children in many situations today. Adam's saviour, the lawyer Ms Roth, is a powerful example of the need for advocacy to assert the human rights of any oppressed group. In the author's words, she is one of the Permitteds 'who refuse to have their humanity limited'. Her voice can confront injustice from within the system and challenge the legality of Adam's interrogation. This invites us to question our own actions when faced with the abuse of power within our own societies.

Adam's appeal to the foreign visiting violinist also highlights the role of the international community in speaking up for oppressed groups and keeping the spotlight on the actions of intolerant regimes.

Martha thought the level of this book's language was aimed at the 10-12 age group, but that the issues raised need some discussion. She said, 'you need a level of awareness of History and Politics to fully process this book,' and I agree. This book would be an excellent class text for years 7 or 8 at Secondary level. While History teachers may be limited by the curriculum, an English lesson may have more freedom to explore the challenging issues raised by the story of Adam and his friends.

Children of the Stone City is a daring book which confronts injustices that blight the lives of far too many children in today's divided world.

Ailish D'Arcy
With contributions from Martha Elston

Edith Summerskill

Mary Honeyball, *Edith Summerskill – The Life and Times of a Pioneering Feminist Labour MP*, Bloomsbury, 288 pages, 2022, ISBN 9781350252425, £25

Mary Honeyball's carefully researched biography of Dr Edith Summerskill is important and well timed. The COVID pandemic has scared and humbled us, as we found ourselves so dependent on the teams of doctors, nurses and ancillary workers in the National Health Service, who we celebrated with painted hearts on notice boards and clapped every Thursday for OUR NHS; a service free for everyone, from cradle to grave; Prime Minister to the poorest homeless person living on the streets of a city or in the Outer Hebrides. The NHS epitomises the radicalism of the post-war Labour Government led by Clement Attlee, and personified by Nye Bevan. Yet the outspokenly feminist contribution of Dr. Edith is seldom acknowledged.

Edith Summerskill is written with natural empathy and admiration and uses a broad historical focus. Mary Honeyball's many years in the Labour Movement have been especially focused on issues of gender equality. As an elected Member of the European Parliament from 2000 to 2019, she served on and became vice-chair of the Women's Rights and Gender Equality Committee. This gives the book insight and personal meaning, whilst its celebration of the post-war administration is a reminder of the power of government to become the agent of lasting change and reform when new, politically-driven ideas are linked to their swift implementation. It was a fascinating time to live through.

My own mother was herself a great admirer of Dr. Edith Summerskill, not least because she was one of the earliest trained health visitors in the 1920s. She appreciated Edith's outspoken clarity in prioritising key pieces of legislation. For example, The Milk (Special Designations) Bill became law in May 1949. It decreed that all retail milk had to be sold with designations that indicated it was free of tuberculosis (TB), or 'TT tested', sterilised or pasteurised. In Edith's opening speech she renamed the Bill the 'Milk (Save the Children) Bill' and, on its Royal Assent, referred to it 'with her customary self-belief', says Honeyball, as 'my finest hour'.

Dr Edith Summerskill was married to a doctor, Jeffrey Samuel. Their practice lay in some of the poorer areas of London. Throughout her life, she kept foremost her pride and devotion to her work as a doctor. It directly informed her politics, and Honeyball spells out how she used the self-confidence it gave her to spell out opinions and policy in a very clear, simple way. Never afraid to raise controversial issues, in 1936 she reminded the National Conference of Labour Women that 13 per cent of women died following an abortion. She was not supported, but opposition within official Labour circles never deterred her championing new causes for women rights, whether it was easier access to birth control, which took many years to achieve, treating venereal disease, or when she first ran for a Parliamentary seat in Bury, where she upset a Roman Catholic priest with her views on contraception and abortion.

Well before the outbreak of the Second World War, Edith and Jeffrey joined the newly founded Socialist Medical Association (SMA). They were big supporters of the League of Nations initiatives in the 1930s, as Edith's political ambitions became stronger.

It is striking that she referred to herself as a feminist, in a matter of fact way, decades before this was common in politics at local or national level. There were 11 women Members of Parliament when Edith was first elected in 1938, but only her and Eleanor Rathbone openly accepted and used the term feminist as a description of their views. Their partnership triggered a question which Edith put to the Secretary of Health, in July

1939, as she asked whether a woman, if she requested it, should be allowed an analgesic during childbirth.

Dr Summerskill was certainly eager to make her mark. Mary Honeyball discovered how dejected Edith felt after her maiden speech, and how her friend, Josiah Wedgwood, MP for Newcastle-under-Lyme, passed her a note saying: 'Dear Lady, There are many times in life when courage is the thing that counts — Josh'. In 1941, she published a book entitled *Birth without Fear*. Honeyball paints a picture of a tall, dominant, well-dressed woman, with a fur scarf and hat, not so much flaunting attention, but as a strong woman, one with commanding authority as she made her intentions clear, however controversial they were.

Throughout the war, Dr Summerskill helped lay the foundations of a nationwide health service based on equality, doctor first and politician second. She was powerful and influential because her campaigns were based on professional experience, both as a woman and in general practice. Always with s special focus on women, she brought home the stresses of childbirth and disabilities such as rickets, which especially affected the poor. She got to know Beveridge well and strongly supported his proposal for a children's allowance, which was introduced in 1945. But, as ever, Edith felt it was not strong enough and should be paid directly to mothers. For many, writes Honeyball,

'Dr Edith will always be remembered for her virtually single-handed efforts to establish women in the Home Guard in a fully combative role, and campaigned for them to receive the same compensation as men for war injuries and also for more nurseries so that women could do their bit without having to worry about childcare.'

Above all, Honeyball suggests that:

'Edith put women on the map. Women's concerns — childbirth, breast feeding, care of children, women's pensions, rights for housewives – were now on the political agenda. Between 1939 and 1945, Dr Edith Summerskill made a huge contribution to the struggle for women to be seen as citizens in their own right and to have economic and social equality with men.'

According to Honeyball, Edith got on well with Clement Attlee and must have been disappointed not to be given the Health brief after Labour's massive victory in 1945. Instead, she became Minister of Food, typically threwing herself into the nitty-gritty of government, again bringing her professional background to bear on the job of rationing in order to ensure the very best balanced diet for all. Again, I have memories of my mother's health visitor background and her support of Summerskill despite managing a difficult and not always popular job, as she was labelled the woman who argued that margarine was just as good as, if not more tasty than, butter.

Dr Summerskill was also attracted to the limelight of media and became a regular radio voice on programmes such as The Brains Trust. Parliamentary life and culture meant she travelled more, enjoying new experiences, and making fresh contacts. She badly wanted it to continue. The parliamentarian and politician, rather than the doctor, started to predominate. As with MPs before and since, Parliament becomes seductive.

Edith became an elected member of Labour's National Executive Committee in its Women's Section in 1944. Other colleagues who became MPs and key members of the Attlee Cabinet and Government after the 1945 landslide victory were by then in the limelight. As a senior member of the NEC she inevitably had to 'take sides' in personality as well as political differences. The Labour Party had become deeply divided over nuclear weapons with Nye Bevan leading the left-wing body of opinion. Was she 'left' or 'right' wing; Gaitskellite or Bevanite? Ever loyal to the Party Leader, first Attlee, then Gaitskell, the answer became clear. She found herself, as the incumbent Chair of the Party, dealing with the proposal to remove the Labour whip from Nye Bevan over the government decision to test a hydrogen bomb. Bevan lost the committee decision, and many of her former women colleagues such as Jennie Lee and Barbara Castle never forgave her. Her Parliamentary career had been seriously threatened when boundary changes brought together West with East Fulham in one constituency, whose members chose Michael Stewart rather than Edith to fight the seat. Instead, she was selected for Warrington in 1955 and won, and eventually left the House of Commons in 1961. She accepted a peerage and settled to life in the House of Lords.

Mary Honeyball's book brings these 20 tumultuous years back to life. Despite her valuable work for women's health over those years, it has been Nye Bevan and the NHS, not Edith Summerskill, who has held the stage.

Helen Jackson

One face or two?

Nick Thomas-Symonds, *Harold Wilson: The Winner*, Weidenfeld & Nicolson, 2022, 532 pages, hardback, ISBN 9781474611954, £25.00

Thomas-Symonds is, as I write, Shadow Secretary of State for International Trade. Hence, there is an obvious pro-Labour bias, manifest in his two previous biographies of Clement Attlee and Nye Bevan. Since Wilson is Keir Starmer's political hero – he frequently evokes the 'white heat of technology' speech – this book should do no harm to Thomas-Symonds' Party prospects. However, whatever you think of Harold Wilson, this is a must-read.

The book comprises 20 suggestively titled chapters, framed by Introduction and Conclusion, fortified by 46 pages of end-notes, an 11-page, multi-part Bibliography including electronic courses, serviceable Index, and a handful of photos of Wilson from childhood to farewell dinner with Queen, including the first-ever shot of Prime Ministerial knees (on Scilly Isles beach). It is well written, jargon-free, laced with humour. It is impossible, of course, for a reviewer to check every statement. I note one factual mistake, minor in context, but odd. He mentions (p.282) that Australian Prime Minister Harold Holt had died in office. In fact, Holt vanished mysteriously, his body never found, giving rise to competing theories of accident, suicide, assassination.

In my Nottingham Trot days, I had the standard sectarian contempt for Wilson, an attitude long since transferred to Tony Blair. This volume frequently dwindles into hagiography, a counter blast to such contrary works as *Harold Wilson: The Unprincipled Prime Minister*, edited by Andrew Crines and Kevin Hickson (2016).

Wilson came in for a wide range of abuse, most famously the epigram 'Only two things wrong with Harold Wilson – his face.' LBJ dubbed him a 'con-man' (thanks to his refusal to send British troops to Vietnam whilst, in an example of Doublethink, supporting the war). At a different level, there were the ceaseless insults levelled by television comic character Alf Garnett, though he did commend Harold for smoking a pipe. This was, in fact, something of a stage property; at home, Wilson smoked cigars. Likewise, his famous Gannex raincoat, invented in 1951; Harold wanted to be seen as keeping up with the times.

Ken Coates (predictably absent from the Bibliography) would have loathed this book. He unsparingly denounced Wilson in *The Week* (1964-

68, initially co-edited with Robin Blackburn and, later, by Pat Jordan); in such pamphlets as *The Dirty War in Mr Wilson: Or How He Stopped Worrying About Vietnam and Learned to Love the Dollar* (for the Vietnam Solidarity Campaign); culminating in his voluminous *The Crisis of British Socialism: Essays on the rise of Harold Wilson and the fall of the Labour Party* (1971, with grotesque 'reversible turncoat' cartoon cover). That a Labour author could eulogize Wilson would have been quite beyond our Ken.

Thomas-Symonds does condemn Wilson on occasion, for example on his behaviour over compensation for the Aberfan tragedy (p264). He prevaricates over responsibility for the notorious honours list (dubbed, with Marcia Williams in mind, the 'Lavender List'). Williams, an ultimately enigmatic character, receives an enormous amount of attention throughout the book. Thomas-Symonds rightly disbelieves the claim (once made by herself) that Wilson had an affair with her. He was no womaniser, being a family man devoted to wife Mary who also gets much deserved attention for her poetry (quoting some first-rate examples) and care for Harold as he descended into dementia. When *Private Eye's* 'Mrs Wilson's Diary' (spoof of BBC's venerable Mrs Dale's) was turned into a movie, Wilson took care to edit and censor the script.

Likewise, the author rightly dismisses the rumours and accusations that Wilson was a Soviet agent. This nonsense went back to his early visits to Moscow and praise for Soviet achievements in industry and science — the latter, perhaps in his mind, chiming with his famous 1963 vision of Britain as 'forged in the white heat of this (scientific) revolution,' with which Thomas-Symonds begins his book. Overlooked is how Wilson snubbed Stalin by ignoring a dinner invitation, hardly the act of a fellow-traveller.

Thomas-Symonds admits that Wilson was devious in his dealings with high-ranking colleagues/rivals such as Benn, Bevan, Brown, Callaghan, Gaitskell, *et hoc genus omne*), but reasonably points out they were often the same. Nor did he rival such vituperations as Bevan's famous characterization of Gaitskell as 'a desiccated calculating machine'. Factional infighting is nothing new in the Labour Party. Likewise with the Tories, who do it differently.

The author also concedes that Wilson was, until pushed off it, adroit at sitting on the fence over such key issues as devaluation of the pound sterling, Europe, and nationalization of industries. On this last, impetus was provided by Anthony Crosland's *The Future of Socialism* (1956), which exposed the flaws in traditional nationalization, offering alternative models. Wilson entertained similar notions, but must have disagreed with

Crosland's notorious ambition: 'If it's the last thing I do, I'm going to destroy every fucking grammar school in England'. Wilson's own grammar school education was the catalyst for his outstanding performance at Oxford and multifarious academic achievements and writings, very thoroughly and admiringly described in this book. Here, I ride my usual pro-grammar school hobby horse as one who profited from education at The Lincoln School. This issue goes back to Attlee's 1945-50 term, when 'Red' Ellen Wilkinson bravely defended grammar schools as the best hope for working-class advancement. (The above does NOT apply to Ted Heath.)

Wilson is also let off too lightly regarding the 1966 Seamen's strike (pp234-38). He famously denounced it as the work of 'a tightly-knit group of politically motivated men'. But, as Thomas-Symonds' own narrative shows, the seamen had a very good case, despite the communists.

Thomas-Symonds deals even-handedly with Wilson's long-standing struggles with Ian Smith in Rhodesia, as it was then called, and with the *In Place of Strife* manifesto, where there is much on Wilson's loyal supporter, Barbara Castle.

Chapter 13 is a key one for the laudable achievements of the Wilson years: The Race Relations Acts; legalization of male homosexuality; legalization of abortion; equal pay for women; The Open University (Wilson's pet project). Much of this was the work of Roy Jenkins, nicknamed 'Old Beaujolais' by Wilson (p399).

Wilson facilitated these reforms, whilst privately unenthusiastic about some of them (abortion, perhaps also homosexual law reform). As he insisted, 'the Labour Movement is a moral crusade or it is nothing'.

Morgan Phillips, Labour Party General Secretary, proclaimed that 'the Labour Party owes more to Methodism than to Marxism'. Wilson never forgot the Congregationalist beliefs of his father, Herbert. He claimed never to have read Marx. A trifle disingenuous, surely; Marx must have cropped up in his Oxford Philosophy, Politics and Economics (PPE) course. Perhaps he was too pre-occupied with his 'heavy Latin texts', a subject he chose at school.

There are many definitions of 'Socialism': for easy instance, Herbert Morrison's 'Socialism is what the Labour Party does'. The word frequently tripped from Wilson's lips; it had to.

Reform or Revolution? The Great Divide. British voters have repeatedly demonstrated they have no appetite for Trotskyite-led upheaval. Orwell ('the English revolution', *The Lion and the Unicorn*, 1941) briefly flirted with this fantasy, influenced no doubt by his Independent Labour Party

(ILP) connections. In 1951, the Communist Party of Great Britain (CPGB) in 'The British Road to Socialism' gave it up as a bad job, switching to the parliamentary route, to the fury of such diehards as Edward Upward; cf. my discussion of this in *Spokesman* 127, 2015, pages 96-98.

I recall wandering around a Nottinghamshire mining village trying to flog Gerry Healy's Socialist Labour League's papers. At one house, I was politely rebuffed by a dear old duck with the words,
'Sorry, we're not Socialists, we're Labour.'
Some may feel this equally applied to our 'Arold ...

Barry Baldwin

Lost Parliament

Dianne Hayter, David Harley, *The Forgotten Tribe: British MEPs 1979-2020*, John Harper Publishing, 2022, 320 pages, paperback ISBN 9781739143602

Residents of Rushcliffe in Nottinghamshire, such as myself, voted Labour in European Parliamentary elections and saw at least one Labour Party representative amongst five for the East Midlands Constituency. Otherwise, for Westminster, Ken Clarke was returned for Rushcliffe year after year, until he grew tired of the UKIP-tending Conservative Party. Prior to Jack Straw's European electoral 'reforms' of 1999, which let Farage into the EP, Rushcliffe electors could put their cross beside individual candidates. So it was, in 1989, that we elected Ken Coates as the Member of the European Parliament for Nottingham. In due course, I worked in Ken's constituency office and, during the next decade, came to appreciate how much effective casework went through it.

Representing coalfield areas of Nottinghamshire and Derbyshire, there was a host of environmental issues such as opencast mining, air pollution and associated health problems including childhood asthma; polluted minewaters; as well as industrial emissions including poisonous dioxins in rivers. We raised these issues with the then Environmental Commissioner, Ritt Bjerregaard, and she consistently sent helpful responses indicating which directives addressed which environmental issues. In a good number of cases, the Commission raised our complaints with the UK authorities. When Michael Meacher became an environmental minister in Tony Blair's first government in 1997, we found an ally who was able and willing to respond constructively to our concerns raised via Commissioner

Bjerregaard. So it was that the long process of environmental remediation of our old coalfield areas advanced somewhat.

I recount this story to illustrate how hands-on in their constituencies MEPs could be. Brexit has removed that democratic option from people in Britain, along with their European Union citizenship. MEPs and Commission officials are no longer required to respond to communications from Britons, as their status as EU citizens has been annulled. In addition, there is no longer external scrutiny by the Commission of adherence to European directives by the authorities in Britain. So, for example, we see bathing waters in Cornwall discoloured with untreated sewage. Surfers Against Sewage no longer carry their wet suits and boards to rue Wiertz in Brussels to lobby their MEPs about this illegal and unnecessary environmental pollution, with its serious implications for inshore fisheries. Britain's political and democratic decline is deepened by the removal of its cohort of Members of the European Parliament.

The Forgotten Tribe assembles 35 contributions from diverse hands on aspects of European Parliamentary experience ranging from Caroline Lucas on the environment, David Harley's affectionate essay on John Hume, to Alan Donnelly on German Reunification. As Donnelly wrote in *European Labour Forum* magazine in winter 1990-91, 'the fall of the Berlin Wall ... precipitated changes in the post-war political structure of Europe which no political commentators could have foreseen'. Actually, some in Germany and elsewhere had been working towards reunification for some years; it was one of the reasons why the Soviet Peace Committee bitterly criticised preparations for the second European Nuclear Disarmament Convention in Berlin in 1983. Several END activists were elected to the European Parliament in 1989, including Ken Coates, Peter Crampton and Michael McGowan. Glyn Ford was already there.

George Parker, political editor of the *Financial Times*, recalls his years as Brussels correspondent among the 'lost tribe' of British MEPs. He would break bread with Nick Clegg, newly elected in 1999. The FT might cover some developments in the Parliament, but most British media ignored it and had little if any experience of the place or the people elected to sit in the hemicycle. Their indifference and occasional contempt for the European Parliament was shared by not a few Westminster politicians. Tony Blair, I think it was, who let slip his view that the EP was a 'Micky Mouse' Parliament. One of the strengths of *The Forgotten Tribe* is that it explains the detailed nature of European Parliamentary work in scrutinising, refining and amending legislation proposed by the Commission and contrasts that with ways of working at Westminster.

There is much praise for British diplomacy and initiative within the European institutions for the 40 years that the UK was part of what has become the European Union. But that was then. Now, Britain struggles in evident decline, exacerbated by the departure of many EU nationals and their partners who no longer feel welcome here. Tough choices lie ahead. Glyn Ford addresses some of these in the final chapter of *Riding Two Horses: Labour and Europe*, published by Spokesman in 2022 (see Spokesman 152 and below). Britain urgently needs honest and informed debate about the European Union in order to rebuild relations on firm foundations.

Tony Simpson

Into the war zone

Yevgenia Belorusets, *Lucky Breaks*, Pushkin Press, 2022, 198 pages, £9.99, ISBN 9781782278726
Serhiy Zhadan, *The Orphanage*, Yale University Press, 2021, 324 pages, £14.99, ISBN 9780300243017
Andrey Kurkov, *Grey Bees*, Maclehose Press, 2022, 352 pages, £9.99, ISBN 9780857059352
Andrey Kurkov, *Diary of an Invasion*, Mountain Leopard Press, 2022, 304 pages, £16.99, ISBN 9781914495847

Yevgenia Belorusets' urban fairy tales distil hope from the extraordinary lives of ordinary women – florists, midwives, manicurists, hair stylists, cosmetologists, cleaners, assembly line workers – in Kyiv, Donetsk, Antratsyt, Dnipro and elsewhere across the wider terrain of her work as a photojournalist in Post-Soviet Ukraine. Like the two most recent novels of Kurkov and Zhadan, *Lucky Breaks* belongs to the period separating the onset of separatist hostilities in the Donbas and the annexation of Crimea from the fully-fledged invasion of 2022, but it also builds upon her longer project representing 'vulnerable' groups and minorities, LGBTQ, Roma, the low paid and unemployed: except that now her protagonists come tasked, practically and psychologically, with the additional urgencies of 'the deep penetration of traumatic historical events into the fantasies and experiences of everyday life'. Part sociology, part *vox pop*, part magic realism, the rapidly interwoven encounters of Belorusets' thirty-something narratives are designed to allow each woman to stand her ground, to resist in the name of a greater imaginative freedom what the Norwegian novelist

Karl Ove Knausgård has recently called the 'Imperialism of the Absolute ... This is what the novel [or fiction] does: it pulls any abstract conception about life, whether political, philosophical or scientific in nature, into the human sphere, where it no longer stands alone but collides with myriad impressions, thoughts, emotions and actions' [*New Statesman*, Oct-Nov 2022].

If, therefore, *Lucky Breaks* is a war text, it's a radically unconventional one, the belligerents dismissed to the margins with only a single, arguably patriotic reference, fifty pages in, to the ongoing conflict – 'July 5, 2014. Strelkov's forces were leaving Slavyansk' – and scattered images, that go unexplored, of roadblocks, broken, empty streets, a heroism-seeking Ukrainian soldier whose 'company sat in dugouts for two months' intermittently playacting a carnage they, and we, never see: 'only after a few hours of such battling, which never resulted in casualties, would they fall into the sweet sleep of children'. The collection's two opening stories, about a 'gorgeous, perfect woman' – the *doyenne* of the neighbourhood – who leaves a needle, lethally, in the breast of her nightshirt, and her dark twin from Kharkiv, whose childbirthing methods and other idiosyncrasies earn a reputation for unmitigated evil, seem to step straight out of ancient folklore rather than any modern inferno: they emphasise solipsism and 'phantasmagoria', women as the administrators, for good or ill, of their own ways of existing, whatever the external forces bearing down on them. Many are indeed refugees from the war zone, all are shown, as Belorusets' ever-widening critique unfolds, to suffer from forms of entrapment characteristic of the economic system and gender relationships in her society as a whole. The pathos attending their responses can be overwhelming: one woman tethers herself to a bench in Independence Square, the site of the Maidan uprising, renouncing all but the barest contact with a history that consigns her to this subordinate role: right on cue, 'A *person* carried three bouquets past the woman and threw one of them to her. He threw the bouquet as if her were throwing a bone to a dog'. Her sarcastic retort, 'I am a living monument ... but a monument that is soft, unstable and wobbly' recalls Taras Schevchenko's 'Kateryna', the village girl whose all-too-female susceptibility made her emblematic of 19th century servitude. Another woman wrestles, Chaplin-fashion, with a broken [man's!] umbrella she continually casts aside and rescues as if it were the only remaining confirmation of her personal tragedy, of the 'pain, anxiety and fear' invested in her 'wartime habits, her wartime tricks of desperate relations with objects, things, the streets'. Residual empowerments like these betoken an individual dignity the standard routes and nostrums — beauty treatments, horoscopes, oneiromancy, lucky charms (archaic 'Trypillian'), cults and gurus (here Eco-Buddhist) or a bludgeoning entrepreneurial self-glorification ('the most successful person in a city populated by losers') — conspicuously lack.

But there are instances, too, of a social assertiveness and sense of self-worth ready to redefine, at a stroke, the accepted channels of femininity: a florist in Donetsk 'entirely unsuited to real life …it was only inside her store that she knew how to exist', joins the partisans; a young woman slips the leash of her mother's lifelong advocacy of and expertise in ribbon-making and moves from Manganese to Dnipro to find an identity of her own; workers at the Pyramid Salon in Antratsyt are credited (a rare excursion into political satire), against all the odds, with leading a rebellion of 'other local hairdressing establishments, a fitness centre and two supermarkets' against the constant jockeying for control of their city-state in and beyond the Luhansk People's Republic, military interventions and acts of secession, questions of 'patronage and influence' that have 'lost all meaning for them'.

Lucky Breaks draws a magic circle around all its voices, far, at least temporarily, from the elemental chaos driving the narrative of *The Orphanage* or the lethal history viscerally re-enacted in Zhadan's early poem on the 'Executed Renaissance' of Ukrainian intellectuals in the 1930s – 'long ago fragments of hot lexemes / grew cold in mouths filled with fear' – or the bullet fired by a Russian soldier into the head of Schevchenko in Borodyanka in April 2022: 'where death begins', Zhadan avers, 'literature ends'. 'Living orphaned on earth', for Schevchenko, was a compound of serfdom, exile, and a longing for national sovereignty redeemable only by force of arms – the stranded, terrorised, fugitive civilians of the Donbas whose halting, ragged progress across the war zone we follow in Zhadan's novel seem incapable of anything more than an uncomprehending, animal-like endurance. The reader is locked into a sensorium of the body and its negotiation of a wrecked, detritus-filled landscape ruled by marauding, barely differentiated aggressors, survival 'in the crosshairs', from moment to moment, as incalculable as the outcome of a soldier's casual placing of a hand grenade on a barroom counter: 'all they can do is watch it roll slowly, very slowly, towards the edge, pause, roll over the edge, and plunge to the floor'.

Threaded through the relentless accumulation of atrocities – the insistence on comprehensiveness, on rendering every detail of the shattered physical environment and the dehumanising of its inhabitants (he 'leaves no stone unturned and no maggot lonely', as Harold Pinter said of

Beckett) can be overwhelming – is one man's progress towards something like a countervailing moral affirmation. It's *his* body that registers, like a seismograph, every tremor in the unceasing war of attrition, every flashpoint on the horizon ('as if someone's using power tools behind thick curtains'), that flinches at every speculative movement of a Kalashnikov or T-64, that cowers into the deepest hole in a bombardment. In this sense he's utterly representative, although never indifferent, even *in extremis*, to the fates of others, appalled by what he encounters of a widespread callousness – 'No pity for anyone, anyone at all' – an assessment, on Zhadan's part, of the durability of social ties that harbours few illusions. Pasha's decision, in the family home, on the edge of the conflict, to rescue his nephew from a besieged city in occupied territory is merely the precursor of a series of assumed responsibilities and humanitarian impulses always waiting to happen, as if the 'blood-drenched man … crying out to him from the [TV] screen, to no avail' represents, his first instinctive disavowal notwithstanding, a reality of suffering and call to a wider involvement impossible to set aside.

War's inexorable presence is felt, too, but less apocalyptically, in *Grey Bees'* fictional Little Starhorodivka, in the Donets Oblast, with its two remaining incumbents on bombed-out, adjoining streets, 'frenemies' across the political divide, Kurkov employing the same monochrome slow-burning narration familiar from 'Death and the Penguin's' laconic portrayal of innocents adrift in the endemic lawlessness of 90s Kyiv. A corpse in the garden, a Ukrainian soldier shot bearing Christmas gifts to children in nearby Svitle, elicits outrage and compassion but it's Sergeyich's concern for the health and productivity of his hives that alone has the power to prise him loose as spring approaches from the hermit-like satisfactions of candle, clock, 'potbelly' stove and a silence 'like a huge bottle of thick glass'. Sergeyich's Odyssean wanderings in search of a conflict-free sanctuary take him to what he at first perceives to be paradisal surroundings – the Zaporizhzhian hinterland where 'southern Ukrainian drivers … would stop and pick up ripe orange apricots from the grass' and a fairytale, democratised Crimea, 'the air ring[ing] with countless unseen bells … where every living thing – every tree, every vine – has its own voice'. In reality they constitute, like Pasha's story, a political and cultural education, the discovery at every stage of the inescapable human cost of territorial violation and occupation – a community kneeling by the roadside in their hundreds to mourn a murdered son, lost defending the integrity of the Donbas; the frenzied assault on his own person of a traumatised ex-conscript and self-appointed 'counter-terrorist'; the ruthless policing and ethnic hatred of Tatar Muslims administered from Bakhchysarai ('They want to break us') in preparation for a second Soviet-style cleansing; finally, and conclusively, the attempted militarisation of the apiary itself. Sergeyich's transformation into a pro-Tatar activist looks forward, in its inevitability, to the Kurkov of the *Diary of an Invasion*, unashamedly polemical from the Snake Island postage stamp that graces its cover to the (purportedly) samurai epigram with which it ends: 'If you sit on the riverbank for a long time, then sooner or later the corpse of your enemy will float past you downstream'.

One may have doubts about a Manicheanism which repeatedly excoriates a herd mentality that 'still holds the Russian Federation hostage', a people 'writ[ing] gloatingly on their social networks' of war crimes committed in their name while Ukrainians bask in an individualism going all the way back to the 16th-17th century hetmanate: about the intensity and urgency of Kurkov's attachment to cultural and literary expression as such – 'the invisible armour of the human soul' – none. In the short term, however, he writes in May 2022, with no echoing Zelensky, 'every representative of any creative profession must work for their country and for victory in this war'. Belorusets' own 'War Diary', available online and in print by March 2023, matches his in renouncing fiction-making entirely but with a greater emphasis, like her stories, on the personal need contained in any activity designed to offset catastrophe, such as the one she searingly characterises on February 24 as being visited on 'everything human … [the] great common space where we live and hope for a future'. 'Cleanliness', she wryly concedes of her own ritual attachment to housekeeping, 'is a must in a dark room with taped windows'.

Stephen Winfield

Viva Cuba

Richard Hollis and J S Tennant, *Cuba '62–Preludes to a World Crisis*, Five Leaves, 2022, illustrated, 108 pages, ISBN 9781910170991, £11.99

Richard Hollis was in Cuba in 1962. He spent several weeks there in August and September, departing before the nuclear missile crisis between the Soviet Union and the United States unfolded in October. He had travelled to Cuba because he was curious about 'an attempt to build a new society'. Whilst there, Richard wrote to his wife, Tasha, in London, kept a diary, and took photographs (some of which he, regrettably, discarded). These items are the 'inspiration behind this collage of texts and images' which form *Cuba '62*. In fact, Richard had made his own collage on return to London in 1962, entitled *I, Eye*. It was a folded broadsheet of some 48 panels conveying his impressions of Cuba in the early years of the Revolution, which he gave away or sold for a penny. Sixty years later, he has designed and laid out this elegant and evocative record of those tumultuous times.

Bertrand Russell was also curious about Cuba and engaged with what was happening there in 1962. As the world was informed by the US about Soviet missile emplacements on the island, Russell went into overdrive. From a rural post office near his home in North Wales, he telegrammed Presidents Kennedy and Khrushchev, as well as U Thant, Secretary General of the United Nations. On 23 October, Russell telegraphed Kennedy saying:

> *'Your action desperate. Threat to human survival. No conceivable justification. Civilised man condemns it. We will not have mass murder. Ultimatums mean war. I do not speak for power but plead for civilised man. End this madness.'*

To President Khrushchev, Russell was more supplicant:

> *'I appeal to you not to be provoked by the unjustifiable action of the United States in Cuba. The world will support caution. Urge condemnation to be sought through United Nations. Precipitous action could mean annihilation for mankind.'*

Russell had been corresponding with Khrushchev since late 1957, when he addressed his open letter about nuclear peril to the Soviet President and President Eisenhower of the United States. It began 'Most Potent Sirs' and was published in the *New Statesman* on 23 November 1957. Khrushchev responded relatively swiftly, sending his reply to the *Staggers* on 7 December with a request that it be published. John Foster Dulles, US Secretary of State, eventually replied on behalf of President Kennedy, and his letter appeared in the edition of 8 February 1958.

Thereafter, Russell maintained his correspondence with Khrushchev. He had been vehemently opposed to Stalin and the conduct of the Soviet Union under him. But he detected a change of direction under Khrushchev and was able to intervene with him on individual cases of political repression and, in particular, on behalf of Soviet Jews who wished to go to Israel. Such interventions, often with positive outcomes for the individuals concerned, continued until Khrushchev was removed in 1964, when the Soviet authorities became much less responsive.

Returning to October 1962, Russell discovered that Khrushchev had replied to his telegram entreaty when the press rang him in the middle of the afternoon of 24th October. In a three page letter, Khrushchev said:

> '... I understand your worry and anxiety. I should like to assure that the Soviet government will not take any reckless decisions, will not permit itself to be provoked by the unwarranted actions of the United States of America and will do everything to eliminate the situation fraught with irreparable consequences which has arisen in connection with the aggressive actions of the United States Government.'

What aggressive actions had Khrushchev in mind? In addition to US military and covert actions against Cuba itself, Khrushchev also had in mind the positioning of US nuclear armed missiles in Italy and Turkey, within striking distance of Soviet territory. Such forward deployment was apparently an attempt by the United States to reassure NATO allies in Europe. So the nuclear escalatory wheel turned. As recorded in *Cuba '62*, it was the secret US pledge to Khrushchev to remove nuclear-armed missiles from Turkey that unlocked the solution to the Cuban Missile Crisis.

Cuba '62 is particularly poignant about the Soviet missile deployments manned by Ukrainian forces. Many soldiers in these specialist units came from Ukraine, 'for the most part east of the Dnieper', as J S Tennant tells us in his Postscript. The nuclear conundrum continues to plague us, both east and west of that big river, and much further afield in Europe.

Cuba '62 is timely and distinguished publishing from Five Leaves Publications in Nottingham, a UNESCO City of Literature. Uniquely illustrated and beautifully printed, it evokes Cuba's hopes in the early years of its vibrant Revolution.

Tony Simpson

European Parliamentarian

Glyn Ford, *Riding Two Horses – Labour in Europe*, Spokesman, 2022, 400 pages, paperback ISBN 9780851249070, £14.99

In nearly 400 pages of densely packed stories, anecdotes and philosophical reflections, Glyn Ford recounts his 50 years plus of political activity, including his 25 year period as a prominent Member of the European Parliament. It is a rich tapestry, illustrating the multiple ways in which he engaged in politics. Ford rode the two horses — Labour and Europe — in multiple venues extending well beyond Britain and Brussels.

Besides some personal history and tales from youthful travels, the book covers the main political fields in which Ford played a significant role. Besides the European Parliament, with which they are interwoven, they include local government in Tameside; science and science policy; the intricate politics of the two Koreas, Japan and China; challenging election monitoring in several countries; intricate factional battles in the Labour Party; and fighting the far right across Europe. It is all written with an eye to important or amusing details, while setting out the wider contexts and implications.

Ford served as an MEP for 25 years (from 1984 to 2009), during which time he was for four years the UK Labour Leader in the European Parliament and a Deputy Leader of the wider Socialist Group of MEPs — then the largest in the Parliament. This was a period of historic change, as the Parliament was transformed from essentially a consultative forum into a proper legislative chamber whose approval is now required for (almost) all European Union legislation, its budget, international agreements signed by the EU, and the appointment of the European Commission and its President. It was also a time of change in the Labour Party and in the trade union movement, when previous divisions and opposition to Europe gave way to widespread acceptance of, and even some enthusiasm for, the project. The role of Labour MEPs, including Ford himself, in this evolution is covered in some detail. Indeed, he himself was originally an 'anti-marketeer', but soon became convinced that leaving Europe would be costly and damaging for Britain, while reforming Europe was possible and offered many opportunities to the Left. Labour's shift was relatively rapid, but not smooth, and Ford recounts a number of incidents and battles fought, and sets out his sometimes trenchant views of the various Labour figures and leaders involved.

Ford served over time on various Parliamentary committees, and describes his role on them and the issues they faced. They include the committees on Energy, Research & Technology (where his scientific background could be usefully deployed, in a context that became highly political with Reagan's 'Star Wars' proposals); International Trade (a major EU competence, with both economic and geopolitical implications); and Foreign Affairs (not least during the convulsive period of the Iraq war). In his first term, he was elected chair of a Committee of Inquiry into the Growth of Racism and Fascism in Europe and in the next Parliament became the rapporteur for a follow up Committee of Inquiry into Racism and Xenophobia, in the process becoming one of Europe's greatest experts in the field and a target of far-right attacks.

Ford's extra-European activities, not least in East Asia, whether as part of official EP delegations or as a freelancing networker, take a large chunk of the book. His behind-the-scenes contributions to defusing crises on the Korean peninsula make for fascinating reading. His deep knowledge and wide network of contacts in the two Koreas, Japan (where he was a university lecturer in his twenties), and China make these sections of the book a must read for anyone interested in the area and are highly relevant today. His account of EU electoral observation missions in Indonesia show that such missions can sometimes really play an important role.

Riding Two Horses is organised in ten chapters, each with substantial endnotes citing sources, has a select bibliography and a substantial index. Anyone interested in any of the subjects it covers will find much of interest, from perceptive historical explanations, to blow-by-blow accounts of events. It is dense: some sections read as if whole paragraphs had to be condensed into single sentences to cut the page count. It is demanding: some fields require a high degree of prior knowledge to fully understand. It is blunt: Ford can be acerbically dismissive of some of his colleagues. It is entertaining: he has an eye for good anecdotes and yarns. And it is a contribution to the historical record of what British MEPs did and achieved in the European Parliament.

Richard Corbett

Subscribe to *The Spokesman*
Journal of the *Bertrand Russell Peace Foundation*

The Spokesman is the journal of the Bertrand Russell Peace Foundation. It features independent journalism on peace and nuclear disarmament, human rights and civil liberties, and contemporary politics.
**Founded by Bertrand Russell,
Edited by Ken Coates 1970-2010.
Edited by Tony Simpson and Tom Unterrainer.**

Spokesman 152
Proliferate Peace

Spokesman 151
Our Common Security

Spokesman 150
Bertrand Russell 150

Spokesman 149
No Drone Zone

Spokesman 148
Counting WMD

Spokesman 147
Challenging Nuclearism

**Subscribe | 3 issues per year | Individuals: £20 UK, £25 RoW
Institutions: £33 UK, £38 Europe, £40 RoW**

www.spokesmanbooks.org